Civilised Society

Uncivilised Events in Civilised Society

Ambrose Onyekwere

authorHOUSE®

AuthorHouse™ UK Ltd.
500 Avebury Boulevard
Central Milton Keynes, MK9 2BE
www.authorhouse.co.uk
Phone: 08001974150

First published by AuthorHouse 2/17/2010

ISBN: 978-1-4389-2230-0 (sc)

This book is printed on acid-free paper.

This book is dedicate to the memory of my late
mother, Mrs F. C. Onyekwere

Contents

Author's Note

What makes a civilised society – the people in it? It is tempting to think of bad behaving in civilised society as them being uncivilised society for the purpose of this book. As with most uncivilised societies, is what people do within a given society that makes them uncivilised society? 'Uncivilised issues at the civilised societies what is civilisation then?' A book that changes the way we see civilised society because when it comes to matters of the living, working and getting promotion in Britain between whites and ethnic minorities, things differ and look suspicious that is why I am writing this book. 'Ethnic minorities want trust, not support from white British.' Believe it or not, there are some white and ethnic minority people behaving in an uncivilised manner in civilised societies. I own a special debt to all people and community involved in this book as a novel is not the achievement of a single individual – the author.

Introduction

Story of civilisation, civilised society and uncivilised society – uncivilised issues developing in a civilised society then what is civilised society? A man left Africa for Britain to learn good and civilised behaviour but ended up learning nothing good other than cunning behaviour. A story of some unaccepted behaviour and uncivilised events in civilised Britain in the 21st century. Examples of Professional qualified workers who cannot get professional jobs positions because of their colour or accent, suggests 'discrimination' and exposes lapses in the British society as some unqualified Britons are getting better jobs that are supposed to be for qualified workers via connection. After living in Britain for more than 10 years with more uncivilised events coming up in each given day like shootings, stabbings, divorces, prostitution, human trafficking, teenage parenthood, alcoholism, and drug abuse etc. The story is asking if we have

1

civilised individuals in a given society and not a civilised society.

Search for civilised Society

Ancient issues are alive and thriving alongside modern civilised society, what is civilised society then? 'Some people behave like they are years behind in life in a civilised society, yet they feel superior and superimpose against people from ethnic minority group.' Broken civilised society with bitter divorces, yobs culture and greed, Britain community disability problems are serious, urgent and growing, I am becoming depress as things going from bad to worse. Why some mums, dads and children bombarding each other with foul language on the street, at home, at work and in the public place in civilised society – why having barbaric behaviour in a civilised society, what is civilisation then? What is civilised society with uncivilised issues happening in civilised society? Do we have civilised individual in a given society not civilised society? Why people in civilised societies are developing and behaving in an uncivilised manner in civilised societies, what is civilised society then? For more than 10 years I have lived in civilised society, I have seen uncivilised issues happening in a civilised society. Can civilised society also have uncivilised people? 'When is Europe and United States of America civilised society not civilised?' Europe and United States is well known for the high standards of its living conditions. While this is something to be proud of, it can also create its own problems and disappointments for parents who are unable to secure a place for their child higher living condition. The reality is that, 'in civilised society today, there are growing numbers of dysfunctional parents with complex and multiple problems, many children with multiple and complex need too.' Now, some group of people in civilised society are looking for better ways to make life better for themselves like 'a wife deceived husband into bringing up her lover's kids, Briton mum secretly cheated on tycoon husband for six years and end up having children with lover – but the real victims are the kids.' With British society having many schoolboy/girl dads and mums in civilised society with the hope of getting the state benefit for payment of bills, buy baby nappies, clothes and make sure they have some food at home. Now, in civilised society, prison is heaven for some people, 'prison inmates are better fed than people in hostel, hospital or at home. Jail food is very healthy, well prepared by professional qualified chefs and varied.' We have some lost generation of youths as some people prefer to live inside prison by committing petty crimes. Why having healthy generation of young people in civilised society with no toilet train – teens from split parents becoming teen dads and mums, becoming single parents too because of lack of cash, no successful careers and having behavioural problems. British teens leaving college to become hook on a life of welfare dependency and criminality. What a Broken Britain – school teen mums and dads also from single parental family becoming single dads and mums too are becoming fashionable. 'Mums children as most of the teen parents carry teen-children and becoming single parent too are from single mum's families as eight out of ten those children are from family home headed by women in a civilised society.' Single teen school parents looking for higher state benefits are becoming lifestyle and club in a civilised society, whatever, you do in a civilised society seems to be the most civilised manner of doing things, why? No Alcohol. No Smoking signs – it is against the law to smoke anywhere on these premises, yet you see workers and workers drinking and smoking in the same premises. Why are we having some people in civilised society with no home training in a civilised society?

Civilised and rich society like London city government councils with too many responsibilities, including fighting the drugs trade, alcohol fuel violence, rape cases or sex crimes, racial and discrimination problems, stopping Londoners making/selling fake DVD and CD's, frauds, junk food problems, problem concerning black magic, love voodoo, business transaction, and court cases, even some people obstructing moving train and bus doors. Why are so many of my fellow Britons breaking the ultimate taboo of civilisation – civilised people behaving badly in civilised society? This bad behaviour is not isolated issue but everybody in the city knows about it yet nothing is being done by the individual concerned to correct their mistakes. Parents should advise their family members about good behaviour and you will be surprised the result or effect of your advice on your children future behaviour. Our future is in our hand. In addition, London dirty street pavements caused by fast food, chewing gum, and cigarette ends litter, dogs fouling, looking at the street pavements I just felt frustrated and embarrassed. However, it should be them who should be feeling embarrassed for littering the streets. Why is London a city of litterbugs, I ask myself? Why is the city pavements dotted with chewing gum? Where has the civilised society gone? What is civilisation? Why street alcohol and drug dependency rough sleepers in a rich and civilised society streets? Street homeless people in a civilised society why? More than 11,000 under-16-year addicted children in England getting help for addiction to drink or drugs, and Britain, the cocaine capital of Europe – according to the UN World Drug Report of 2009. '22 Britons face death penalties over drugs offences in foreign jails and drugs trade take desperate turn in Britain when some imported children sweets were filled with cocaine.' Alcohol drink is also a major factor in the number of British people getting into trouble on holiday or needing hospital treatment. 'More than one million Britons are alcohol dependent and the annual cost to the British National Health Service is £2.5 billion and almost 100,000 people will drink to death over the next decade because of cheap alcohol.' 'Can't civilised individual know what is good and bad for their body? Drugs and alcohol abuse making people to be street homeless in civilised society, why?' Nightmare of drugs, yobs, gangs, thugs, organised crime or thieves sickening our streets, and football fans culture causing criminal damage and incites violence to our society. Over the past 10 years, violent crime has jumped nationally by close 70 percent – violence in the British society has become a norm and not an exception. A British 'prison officer jailed for selling drugs to prisoners, a prison officer becomes a prisoner', a culture of carelessness seen in an uncivilised society now in a civilised society – why? About 1.45 million – the number of vehicle related thefts that were recorded in 2007/08. In addition, the number of working age adult claiming benefits instead of working is 6 million – so UK real jobless adults figure is 6 million. There are now 4 million Britons of working age living in a home where no one has a job, why is a civilised society having uncivilised issues? Politics is a dirty business even in civilised society – UK members of parliament corruption, 'politicians expenses scandal', parliamentary member's claimed money on home mortgages that did not exist as seen in uncivilised society of third world nations. About £2 billion tax credits lost through fraud and office error in Britain, a treasury report figure showed. 'A civilised society collecting uncivilised issues instead of civilised issues, then what is civilised society?' Should a civilised society like London city be fighting issues related to bad behaviour in the 21st century? What is civilised society then? Moreover, from other civilised societies like America, France, Russia, and Germany behaving in uncivilised manner, 'disgusting release of images of abused Iran prisoners by the United States military.' 'Civilised Russia society traditional alcohol abused and bottle problem.' 'Spanish bull bloody run festival – ancient skills are alive and thriving alongside modern society then what is civilised society?' 'The Los Angeles tradition bum's rush – fans line up to show their bums to the speeding trains.' 'Sickening boasts of America's monsters 'husband and wife' who allegedly kidnapped an 11-years- old girl and held her captive for 18 years – the girl had her first daughter with the man when she was just 14 and the second daughter four years later.' When all the civilised society government targets have been unrealistic to maintain a well-behaved society then what is civilised society? Where is the real civilised society with a lot of uncivilised behaviour in civilised societies, please mind your manners. I have seen civilised society, good, bad, and ugly sides of behaviour and now I can read civilised society like a novel. Do we have civilised society or some civilised individual in each given society? Think well behave society, think Africa society.

An innocent person from uncivilised society went to a civilised society to learn civilised behaving manners but ended-up learning nothing good than mess, 'good egg is hit by bad eggs.' To understand any society's behaviour related issues, you have to live there. 'The ugly truth about civilised society is uncivilised issues in civilised society.' So, is a civilised society just a dream? People behaving in an uncivilised manner in civilised societies, what is civilised society then? Do we have civilised individual in each given society that is not a civilised society? Parents prevent society bad behaviour by advising your children and help support your own society today, our community our responsibility – our family housing reflect the state of our society. Why are people behaving in an uncivilised ways in a civilised society? A boss of children charity said, 'babies born to bad parent should be removed from their families as soon as possible to stop them being damaged beyond repair.' So there are bad parents in civilised society – more than 10,000 families with children are suffering from problem of alcohol, drugs and domestic abuse in UK, a study revealed. 'Parents behaving badly in a civilised society, what is civilised society then?' However, 'think well behave children, think parent advice and support.' Where have the societal norms which are inculcated by parents gone with uncivilised issues happening in a civilised society? Parents enlighten up your children as family home is the first centre for all youths needs, because life is more fun when you have well behaved children in a decent home. However, why some people living in great looking society live like people from uncivilised society – still unanswered question about civilisation. It's never bad in civilised society, whatever people do in civilised society is a civilised manner of doing things. Even when it's bad it's never bad in civilised society. Why can't people in civilised society be at home in a world of opportunity – Free State money via benefit? 'Parents advice and support at family home, ways to make children life little easier and good things come to those parents who support family members.'

However, make no mistake about my comment as London city is sure, a lovely place to live. It is better than any Africa city and no African has left London because of the society bad behaviour – Britain is still a heaven as to compare with Africa nations. Millions of Africans have visited UK on holiday, to study or work in the past and over 100,000 Africans visit UK every year now. 'London is a city icon, and an iconic city of the world.' 'More than 1,000 immigrants are still arriving every day to settle in Britain as they have for the past 10 years however, 1,000 a day rate is crazy.' Wish you were in Britain society, African and Asian war zones battle for economic migrants. British government has allowed some people inside the country and some are now asking for allowances from the government in form self benefits. 'People allowed into Britain nation are now asking for Allowance from British government – why?'

In 1992, as Nigeria was returning to democracy from military government and political parties were set up, I was informed that a man living in my council ward would be heading my political party meeting. This man was a London trained, well-behaved person so was I informed.

As we were sitting on the first day of the meeting, a man walked into the meeting hall and took his place at the high table, well dressed in a suit, tie, and boot shoe under the African afternoon sun heat, the hottest time of the day – he was the London educated and trained gentle man. The afternoon was so hot that all the other people for the meeting were wearing t-shirt and polo shirts except the head of the meeting. After ten meetings with the London trained head of our political meeting, I noticed that he was still wearing suit, tie and boot shoe at each meeting, well spoken and well behaved, accountability to his finance expenses and talking.

I lived in Asia countries for five years and had all my university education in Asia. During that time, I behaved and dressed like a Nigerian. Therefore, why was this Nigerian man who was London trained, behaving like a British in Nigeria society always adorning a suit and tie? My friends and other people in the meeting said that, because he studied in London, he was trying to let us know that he is a British educated and trained person. He was trying to tell us that he studied in a civilised society. Therefore, does that mean that my own education and training was from an uncivilised society for not wearing Asia clothes? I ask myself. So should I be coming to political meetings with Asian clothes as an Asian trained graduate as to let people know that I am graduate from an Asian University? I spent five years in India and before I left Nigeria, I was thinking that all the parks and women I was seeing in Indian films in Nigeria would be like the ones I would be seeing on India streets, once I arrived there – I was disappointed. 'The real reality of India films doesn't match the society living romance.'

Why, is this London trained Nigerian pretending to be a British in Nigeria community? I ask myself. I wear polo shirts or t-shirts and jeans because of heat from the sun but he said I had to dress like him

– suit and tie as one of the appointed officers. Later he said that I had to go to Britain or other Western European countries to see civilised culture that is different from Nigeria, India or Asia culture I had already visited. Is Africa society too cool for you wearing t-shirt? Is it fine to wear tie, suit, and boot in Africa afternoon sun heat than, I said to him.

Where is the Nigerian society in 21st century civilisation? We Nigerians have and use digital Cameras, Widescreen TVS, DVDS and VCR machines, Mobile phones, Fast-food shops, iPod and MP3, Wash and Dry machine, Fridge and Microwave, Watch and Clock, Computer and Cars, good houses and good roads. What type of civilisation was this London-trained Nigerian man telling me about Europe? 'I ask myself.' No to his system of dressing and thinking, I must visit Britain – a civilised society to see better ways of behaving myself.

Nigeria, my country – full of corruption and mismanagement means that despite the country's vast oil wealth, about 70 per cent of Nigerians live in poverty with streets looking less than decent – streets full of rubbish. Series of corruption by Nigeria leaders means that modern life in Nigeria is rubbish. Nigerian leaders and top government officials should bury their heads in shame. Corruption is rampant. You even witness on Nigerian streets Police officers stopping vehicles and asking for money without checking the vehicle documents. Corruption so wide open that you have to bid a price with a Police officer before an officer can listen to a case you brought to report. In Nigeria, you will see a public office holder having 5 to 12 private cars and yet no good hospitals for their health treatment – all the top public office holders visit Europe or America for treatment. Therefore, can there be civilisation in a confused society, such as Nigeria? Nigerian public officials declared assets without declaring taxes paid on the assets and main source of getting the assets. I was compelled to move, to see how developed countries look like, and how their working systems operate. Since Asian societies are less civilised than European society and based on the information I received that European countries like Britain are civilised and developed societies; I decided that I was not going to waste time going for a British Visa – a country that ruled my country-Nigeria for years. If you live and work in a society, you will know whether they are well behaved or not. But, if you have not lived in a developed country, all you are told is that, they are societies of good manners, reserved and morally upright – that its streets are full of goodness.

As I was about to leave Nigeria for Britain, I asked questions about the typical Britons' behaviour and was told that Britain is a civilised society and that I would learn a lot from the British society, mostly behaviour. However, informed of Britain's physical discrimination in 1950 by a half brother who was a student in the United Kingdom and white people not sitting near a black person in public buses because 'black people's body and their cooking smelt very badly.' I was then faced with a predicament – a civilised society that discriminates. Then what is a civilised society? Why is there discrimination in a civilised society? Where have the civilised people gone? I asked myself. Can we have uncivilised people in civilised society? I consulted my English dictionary to know the meaning of civilised society and discrimination. All I learnt about civilised society is 'human societies that is out of savagery or barbarism into a state of polite and good mannered refined human being, well educated and enlightened human society with advanced social development and legal organisation.' Discrimination was all about 'unfair treatment of a person or group.' To my simple words, a civilised society must be patient, kind, and not jealous, arrogant or wide. Why does discrimination exist in civilised society? I was going to Britain with these two words, civilised society and discrimination and for an opportunity to change my life – to learn a good civilised behaviour.

As I flew into London-Britain, things were bigger, better and brilliant, as we Africans had been hoping in the political offices in Nigeria. London city on its part had big and good airports, train stations, taxi, supermarkets, and urban buses. London, 'where dream becomes reality.' However, some Britons were arrogant, rude, messy, lousy, uncultured and jealous. 'How can people be sleeping rough at international airport? I become sick with anxiety. My first British friend is a homeless person.' Was this the civilised society we Africans had been hoping to see? Is civilisation just about a society having big houses, roads, and industries? Could there be uncivilised people in a civilised society? 'I come to visit the great behave master British society and instead seeing great arrogant Briton masters.' The news from a free newspaper I pick from the airport is disgusting, 'a study revealed London city as Britain's credit-card fraud capital. In the south-east London, £1 in every £3 spent online is fraudulent, making it the UK's fraud hotspot. Across Britain, it is believed that more than £600m is lost to fraudsters each year – around £1,100 a minute – fraud will keep rising because it is not a police priority – it is big retailers who lose out because they have to refund the credit card companies.' Why an online criminal in a civilised society? However, an advance criminals in a civilised society must be part of the society civilisation, I ask myself.' Also in the same newspaper are, 'a TV star peered into a van and found a man's corpse.' 'A British mum, 41 years old killed her two daughters 14 and 16 years while they slept at her home to ruin her ex-husband's life after being consumed by jealously over his girlfriend.' 'A millionaire landlord murdered tenant to save a £million property deal.' 'Bones found in bag M15 motorway are human, police confirmed.' Bad news in just one free newspaper I pick from the airport. I am sick and worry – uncivilised issues developing in a civilised society, what is civilised society then?

At the airport, I stayed in the airport immigration line for more than three hours before I could see the immigration officer while British passport holders entry points were empty – British officers had no respect for foreigners- especially Africans and Asians I think. At the immigration counter, 'I had an uncomfortable laugh, being in a civilised society and people behaving in an uncivilised manner.' Be faster; treat other people the way you will like to be treated yourself, the British and Europeans counters are empty, treat travellers or visitors well, and makes the world a nicer place to live, I said.

I am doing my work, my country work and rights with no discrimination, said the immigration officer.

But, I am seeing discrimination openly at the airport – no person at the counters for British and Europeans lines, however more than five hundred people waiting at the counters for Asians and Africans lines, can't you see the line, I ask. 'In Africa people with international passport-foreigners counters are always manage well and are empty and why, 'I ask myself - visitors empty counters, a sign of a warm welcome.'

I stayed another five hours with the airport customs as a British Asian custom officer asked and questioned me about hard drugs in Nigeria, saying 'Nigerians are bringing drugs into UK. Nigerians are drug-linking centres. Nigerians are involved in this drug and that drug' – not even a little respect for me but rude and threatening for all Nigerians as follow passengers stood 'frozen in shock.' What kind of future for the Nigerians, I ask myself.

Have you anything to tell me about Nigeria drugs. It will help fight drug problems between UK and Nigeria, said the custom officer.

You are wasting my time, stop it custom officer, I am a foreigner, you are embarrassing your country and yourself, I told the custom officer.

If you say that I am wasting your time again, I will send you back to Nigeria because Nigerians are drug dealers, said the custom officer'

'I then kept quiet as I had waited to get this my Britain entry visa for the past four years.' However, 'I think the British airport workers has put me in my place as a Blackman, I ask myself.'

You can go, the officer said 'after 4 hours and 45 minutes searching my box and my body' or you want me to send you back to Nigeria asked the custom officer.

I looked at his face and had a little bit of laugh with him, but then I had received a little bit of abusive words from him. I then took all my items and ran away for I did not want the customs officer to send me back to Nigeria. 'Could this customs' officer be among Britain's civilised individuals

I asked myself? Who is a civilised individual?' 'Custom officers, think Nigerians are all drug traffickers? Think again.' The officer wanted me seen and not heard. I thought in a civilised society you can talk and express your feeling, if you feel untreated. Why was my complaint becoming a dispute in a civilised society? After about 7 hours inside an aeroplane, other hours at the immigration counters, I am exhausted and dishevelled – why is this custom officer still kept firing unanswerable questions to me, I ask myself.

However, I was comfortable as the sights, sounds and smells of the airport makes me happy – the airport is well planned I said within myself.' 'Why are complaints becoming disputes, in the British society? Certainly a person in a civilised society should be capable of separating complaints from disputes?' I have seen the ugly truths about civilised society; people can have bad manners even in a civilised society. The officer was too rude to be a British citizen as a new comer to British society but the officer claimed that he was doing his normal work. 'If it was now that I am a British citizen, I would have taken him to court for bullying and harassment.' 'It was terrifying, I was speechless. I could not believe that a public official in civilised society can be verbally abusive, I could not move my feet and later used the toilet after leaving the officers counters as to have a good access to myself again as I used to be before I reach the London airport.'

Knowing the airport workers, knowing where I belong. 'Every society has its own problem, Britain or Nigeria as a society has problem too. However, Nigeria bribery and corruption problems seem to have eaten so deep into the fresh of the society that virtually every nation around the globe believes that Nigeria is arguably one of the most corrupt nations of the earth.' The earth belongs not to the rich and civilised nations but to everyone. Fame and powerful society, however, who is going to live forever, my country is not drug producing society? I ask myself. I could not believe the behaviour I am seeing from airport workers – don't they want us, what makes people feel glamorous and superimpose in a civilised society, what did we do wrong?' I ask myself.

Coming to Europe was a difficult task and on reaching Europe, life becomes difficult to live – only deep shock stopped me from going back to Africa. But, 'I love the smell of my success to London city. I love the smell of civilised society.' It is time to rethink, reshape, and restore my living plans – all my life problems solved. 'Wish you were here. Welcome to the brightest society of the world – England a great place to visit, work or live.' However, a civilised society with bad manners – swearing, spitting and queue-jumping, rude Britons as they call them, Britons using racially aggravated threatening, abusive or insulting words and behaviour between white people, ethnic minority group against ethnic minority group, white people against ethnic minority group and ethnic minority group against white people. What a confused society, with re-occurrence of issues related to uncivilised behaviours and events in a civilised society in every given day. 'Uncivilised event in a civilised society what is a civilised society? Where have the civilised individuals gone?' Of course, I was not in Britain just to see tall buildings or different cars on the streets for I have already seen a lot of them in Nigeria. I came to learn in British society; one good attraction of British society for we-Africans and other developing countries is that Britain is a rich, civilised, monarch, with Christian values, and cultured society. Developing countries can never believe that Europe have poor people or petty criminals unless you are in Europe. No African can believe that some British people, the origin of English speaking people cannot speak general Standard English words, which non-British but English-speaking people from other countries can hear and understand. Why some of the English people in England, the birth place of English language cannot write or read English word – JUST SPEAKING ENGLISH. 'An English person speaking English language can never be an achievement in England.'

I had stayed some months in Britain before I started my education. I asked those who studied in London, UK around 1950s about the discrimination in British society and they proposed that the above claims are correct, but I have not read about those 1950s discrimination in any British history notes. In addition, I understood that those British discrimination histories of 1950s are repeating itself. 'Just finish your university course and see, if you will get the same level of job like your white university classmates. You would be pushed to hang your professionally qualified certificate and start doing a lower paid job, that is the only opportunity you will get as a black British man' a 70-years-old black British man told me. 'You are laughing and chattering with the white people now at work and public places however; in the year between 1950 to 1960, black people are seen as an outcast by white people. No white group of people care to talk, laugh or chat with you. Black people talk about anything and everything about their disappointments, dreams, and frustrations in their bedrooms among themselves' he said. However, I've always made the most of my life in London city not in Africa or Caribbean and living here means I still can and you can too. How can I help you son, he asks?

Just to get some information from you about the past UK black history – so it's just no place like native home, think decent living, think native home, I ask?

We were in UK because we didn't have much of a plan, when you have enough money within you please leave, living in UK isn't as much fun as it used to be son, it never been fun living here. 'It is not too good living in London, but it can't be too bad living in London, if you have resource after your university education, it is better you go back to native home and support them', he said.

What is – when you have enough money within you leave to Africa, when is money enough to leave, I asked myself.

'I think if bad events are not mentioned and managed for future generation to study, then history will continue to repeat itself. History seems to be repeating itself, discrimination in Britain's 21st century – a general society in mourning from both European, white, Black, and Asia British etc. Racism and discrimination caused by white British and British-born trying to show-up their supremacy over non-British-born, white British against coloured British-born, coloured British-born against non-British-born.'

After being in London for some months, I called the Nigerian London trained head of our political meetings as I could not see all the British people behaving so well like him. His answer was that, 'I should be a good ambassador of British people once I reached Nigeria as a person who had his education in UK'. 'Be a good ambassador for Britain in Nigeria, you must be joking, I said. I am a Nigerian and should behave like a Nigerian in Nigeria land, I told him'. 'Why was this Nigerian London trained man force pretending that British people are all angels?' I think the stressful and depressive memories in black people's life in London did cause some mentally related issues to you' I told him. 'I have seen some women in London wearing leather hi-leg boots in summer - it is disgusting as this might be caused by either poverty or not having a summer wear. I have seen people in London going to work in jeans depending on the type of work they are doing, while the Nigerian London trained man insinuates that all is good in London – suit and tie. I have seen MP's with battered and worn pair of shoes. I have seen white and coloured British women with their hair covered with dust, I asked them why are they not washing their hair daily and the answer was that her hair would cut if she washes and dries her hair every day. Why this Nigerian London trained man calling Nigerian women 'local women with dirty hairs.'

I later called Nigerian political office workers and informed them about what I was seeing in London. 'They asked how London city as civilised society is. How does British look and behave? What do British men and women like to wear?' London is as good as they use to tell us, the sights, sounds, and smells of a civilised society city differ a lot from uncivilised society cities. However, the ugly truth about London city is the best and worst place to live – it is as bad and as good as you think. Their standard of living was not as easy as we think in Nigeria. A civilised society with street homeless people and some behave more badly than people in Nigeria. 'Unbelievable in my society that a white Briton can be a cleaner, a white man cleaning the street I live and removing my flat rubbish bin bags away. We thought it was the work of black people in London.' I informed them that the British equality behaviour we have been discussing fell below what we have been hoping. Some people behaving in an uncivilised manner in a civilised society, what is civilised society then? We pretend to be perfect as we visit Africa, I said? The Nigerian political office workers informed me about the financial mismanagement of the man I thought to be an angel, the London trained head of our political meetings. I thought the Nigerian London trained man was an angel, physically well dressed but was told about his cunning the local council finance via over-costing contract, he has two full time pay jobs – the local government chairman and a private company director. 'But when compared to local Nigerian politicians who will over cost contract, yet the contract will not be complete and we will not see the money refunded' he is better they said. 'The police were involved but they did not stop the council contracts been given to his own companies, however he becomes police officers best friend', the workers said. So reaching home Africa, I will of course be pretending to be an angel as to be accepted in the community and then start cunning my society's wealth. I learnt a survival idea in Britain. Therefore, 'civilisation is the ability to behave in mature and then cunning ways of getting what you want from individuals or the society.' In Britain too, I have seen contract bidding criminal activities - 112 construction companies rigging bids for contracts. Bidders add money to cost of contract, so successful building firms pay a sum of money to those that lost out, leading to customers having to pay much for construction. About 40-firms have admitted price fixing and 37 others had asked for leniency. In addition, British builders fined £130 million for price-fix scams – several top British building firms received fines running into millions of pounds, after being found guilty of brazen scams to rip off the taxpayers and private developers. The British office of fair trading fined 100 firms a total of £129.5 million for colluding to force up prices paid to build hospitals, schools, universities and housing.

In Nigeria, a contractor pays a sum of money to the top departmental head and political leaders before they get contract; so I have learnt another new idea different from the Nigeria system in Britain. In another incident, a 46-year-old Briton stepped down as a mayor of city after he admitted to magistrates of illegally obtaining money from disabilities benefit. The mayor was secretly filmed overseeing more than 67 pay soccer matches while claiming benefit-white crime, Corruption in civilised society too, I told the political office workers.

What would have British police do different from Nigeria police if this incident happen in UK, they political office workers ask?

In Nigeria, police officers openly extort money from private and commercial drivers on roads, openly asked for private money before registering a case you brought to police station. Nigerian police officers claiming that taking money from individual is not a crime because cost of standard of living is high, I called Nigerian police officers criminals because of taking money from people without issuing a receipt that is been paid to government purse. 'In Nigeria you cannot read the police bad behaviours in the newspaper or the police officers will plan and kill the concern media worker however, in Britain all the police bad behaviour are seen in the newspapers.' In Nigeria, openly extort money from people is called black crime. Therefore, what is wrong when a black person commits black crime?

However in Britain, police officers do not openly commit crime but they commit white crime. A British police inspector 47-years-old awaiting trial for the murder of his 44-years-old wife for having an affair was released on bail after the paying of £200,000 surety by his barrister-brother. The police officer killed himself after apparently shooting his 70-years-old mother-in-law dead, because the 70 years-old woman wanted to testify against the officer for killing his wife and making the killing look like a suicide. The officer's wife, a nurse asked for a divorce and after some days, her body was found at the garage in the family home with a cable tied around her neck and a suicide note lying nearby. A judge admitted that he could not remember why he freed the police officer to kill again while he faces a murder trial. Mr Judge, it must be either black magic from Africa and Asia or bribery in civilised British society of 21st century that made you to free him. 'Still many questions remain unanswered about civilised society police's relationship with courts.' So both Nigeria and British society political office holders and police officers do involve themselves into some forms of criminal activates. 'I do not need to pretend that I have learnt anything good in Britain if I have not. I should be proud of Britain if I am in Britain and be proud of Nigeria once I reach Nigeria.' Does a well-trained Nigerian who has not touched or used vacuum cleaner makes him a dirty or uncivilised family? However, a well-trained Nigerian family call me a civilised person – what is a civilised person? A friend visited my house from Nigeria and I was using a vacuum cleaner for my house's floor rug. To my surprise, neither the well-trained doctor nor his nurse wife had touched or used vacuum cleaner before. His house floor was covered with carpet because of the type of Nigerian climate they have and does not need a vacuum cleaner.

I am 10 years in Europe and Britain without fear or favour and with open mindedness in my view on present modern Britain society of 21st century. How disappointing European and British civilised society are. It is a society with moral standards in decline, binge drinkers and vandalism – knifing, shooting, discrimination and racism, rude and nuisance behaviour (booze British) in words of an 80-years-old white British man I visit as a housing officer. Some Britons call some criminal activities white crime, so a white person committing white crime should not be a problem. British society, which always makes headlines news for the wrong reason – bad issues and criminal events. British villagers bought a car via donation from a local dealer and pays for petrol so police support officer can patrol their neighbourhoods and the police force told the villagers that they could not afford the fuel or they would not be able to police the community – headline news in all the media. An act you see in developing society.

I have noticed that Britain does not have an openly physical discrimination because of government's law against discrimination in Britain but there are still some frictions. Just a little bit of discrimination for instance, a project site with ten staffs all from White Briton. If a person from an ethnic minority becomes the manager, all white staffs will try to abandon the project by taking a long sick leave and refuse attending supervision meetings. White Britons or Britain-born Britons are bent on showing their supreme power as ethnic minority people work with them in Britain. Some project with 98 % of their labour force from one type of ethnic minority people refused taking white British, claiming they cannot work harder than how people from their ethnic minority can. Some ethnic minority British workers refuse to take qualified ethnic minority people as their managers because of fear and reaction of their white British co-workers who would like to be on the top position. Considering some projects are from people from one ethnic minority, white Britons refused working in the project headed by people from ethnic minority. 'A woman who was battered by a Scot for being English says her attacker was let off by police. She was attacked after the thug heard her accent and yelled – go back to England. She suffered two black eyes, a cracked cheekbone and damaged nerves in her eye.' White British killing white British. What a confused society. Irish Britons own organisations in London taking 90 per cent of top and middle managers from Irish people with some of the frontline workers from Ireland descendants, frontline and cleaning workers from other ethnic minority take the remaining 10 per cent labour force – Irish descendants still claim they are from ethnic minority and are therefore being discriminated by English Britons. Asian Britons own organisations taking 95% of their labour force from Asian descendants with the remaining 5% for cleaning and support workers from other ethnic minority. London hospitals full of nurses from ethnic minority group at about 70% but at the management level, there are rarely staffs from the ethnic minority group even when ethnic minority people have more experience and qualification than their co-white Britons.

'It is very simple to monitor equality related issues and discrimination in an urban society like London city by checking an organisation with 90 per cent of its labour force at all level are from one ethnic minority group.' Most of the organisations ran by ethnic minority group take unqualified white Britons as to avoid competition with them and organisation ran by white Britons doing the same to people from ethnic minority group.

In Britain, it is now psychological discrimination – isolation, degradation, denial of reality, denial of power and competency like, not giving equal job positions to people from ethnic minorities in Britain compared to white Britons. I registered in four recruitment agencies, with years of experience and university qualification in housing, but was always called to work as support worker or assistant housing worker by white Briton consultants and was always called for housing officer or housing manager position by African and Asian British consultants. So white Britons calling me for an assistant housing worker jobs only - denial of my competency. 'I think the right step in the direction to avoid discrimination is that the most qualified in the same field they are working should be given top jobs.' What does it take to carry out qualified worker induction? Qualification should be a talent, because there is no known proper way to measure talents or experience without being discriminate against workers and to show some respect to college and university education. 'Ethnic people wait for years before being employed, just killing the black people indirectly until they start developing some behaviour and named as having mentally related issues caused by stress or depression.'

The black British head of the commission for racial equality calls for positive discrimination by the Police, to be allowed to discriminate in favour of hiring British black, Asians and other ethnic minorities in a civilised society. Sir, we are all British and we do not need extra help, remember that Britain is a civilised society, we want equality. The access to working and living system must be equal for everyone – promoting equality, celebrating diversity, and then achieving ethnic minority targets. If I am a qualified graduate in nursing, social science or housing, I want to work in the same position like my co- white Britons and get my promotion when due. If you push black and ethnic minorities group to work above their standard, will you be coming to office to do the work for them?

In 21st century London, when you enter Asian or African supermarkets; you automatically know it belongs to them – overcrowded with items and no space to walk no matter the size of the shop floor. Yet white British shops of the same size remains good-looking. Most of the Asian and African supermarket owners were born in Britain. Therefore it means, it does not matter how long they have lived in Britain, they still remain Asian or African in behaviour in a British society. Is it none availability of fund or cultural behaviour shaping those London Asian and African shops to look like supermarkets in Asian and African cities in Britain? I have come to Britain to see Western and British culture, not to have another African or Asian culture in me. 'Why the reality of going to a civilised society doesn't match the society once you reach?'

British TV station, Big Brother and Shipwrecked programmes in new race row, British newspaper and media claimed. Shipwrecked called black people bad and was for slavery, big brother racial comments on an Asian woman. It is not a new comment or race row to the British society as claimed by British media, Britons do not pretend because the world is watching the TV programmes for names like YID, SPIC, CHAV, SCUM, TOWEL HEAD, RAG HEAD, PIKEY, CHINKY, PAKI, TERRORIST, HALF BREED and NIGGER etc. They are not new comment in the British society. The TV programme comment is not a new race row but shows what an average Briton think about different coloured groups. The TV programme was meant to show how people relate with people from different cultures and we have seen and heard the waiting comments. Never thinks that the controversial comedies are racial; they are just saying what an average Briton think and say about coloured people like 'YOU BLACK THINKING YOU ARE BRITISH BECAUSE YOU ARE BORN IN BRITAIN OR HAVE A BRITISH PASSPORT.' I belief because we have a lot of what I call UNFORTUNATE British - unqualified white workers and coloured Britain-born people who want to be at top position in offices without having the require qualification, people who want better flats and living condition but keep taking state benefits making this country a non-stop moaner society. Some Britons can be so rude and uncultured that you will not believe that some of the Britons are born in Britain society or had live in Britain civilised society for years. 'I am seeing the British culture with some uncivilised events now and having a bit of laughter and a little bit of silly abuses on the British society.'

Britain to enter a new nuclear age, 'whether you like it or not, there'll be new nuclear stations to keep the lights on and nuclear energy will help save our planet – green guru' says government energy review and British minister. Britain building new nuclear power gets all clear, they are intending to meet Britain's twin challenges of ensuring energy supplies, and tackling climate change, Britain's Government said. However, Britain government says no to Iraq, Iran, Korea and some African countries nuclear development. Britain wants uncivilised society to track their climate change problems with technological solution of 17th century but Britain will use 21st century technological solution – nuclear. It's a civilised society that loves everyone in uncivilised society except the uncivilised society that wants to civilise its society. Why discrimination officially within British government practice, policy and procedure system. 'Develop society under-developing developing society. Why?' The law must be equal for everyone, nuclear technology for all the nations, promoting equality, celebrating diversity, and achieving excellent society.

Europe is a civilised society and what about the Eastern Europeans, are they not Europe? Eastern Europeans who behave like the Africans and Asians, who travel and arrive in London with no plans or money and struggle to find work, leaving them with no choice but to sleep rough in parks and toilet rooms, commit crime or rely on state benefit. Eastern European women cradle their children as they sit on London streets begging money and some selling gold rings like women in African and Asian cities. I have come to see European or western culture not African or Asian culture. I have seen different European culture in London city. Eastern European women begging in under and over ground trains like people in uncivilised society. Is London not a civilised society? Why having beggars in London trains? Eastern Europeans knocking at my house door and asking if I want to buy carpet, television, gold rings, 'I do not want smuggled and stolen goods civilised Europeans.' Some Eastern European gangs smuggle illegally, children two to three-years-old from Eastern European poor families into British cities, teach the children how to be a beggar, pickpocket or commit crimes. 'Human trafficking and children abuse in the 21st century Britain's civilised society' what is civilised society then? I am a bit worried about my children's future. Eastern European children visit public places, start cleaning your shoe, crying and asking for money. Sometimes, the children take your items if you do not take care of your property, acts you see in developing countries in Africa and Asia in civilised Britain society. I thought Europeans are civilised people, are those among civilised Europeans.

Britain, a society where bad habits are good news in national media and newspapers – you misuse alcohol, drug or kill, you then become popular, what a shame – 175 robberies at knifepoint a day in Britain, a new report claims and I have registered in my dairy. 'I thought in a civilised society you can go where you want to go when you want, why are we seeing youth killers in the civilised society streets?' A lot of uncivilised behaviours in the civilised society, when will British society back in the picture again? No more tears in the society. About 400 drunken patients are swamping London hospitals casualty departments per week despite massive campaigns to cut binge drinking. Why can't people from civilised society know what is not good for their body? Africans are watching Britain's TV broadcasting, reading newspapers and internet where celebrities are glamorising cocaine use and fuelling problems in Africa, celebrities still receive lucrative contract even after being photographed sniffing. Britain, the internet is on and has no boundary. Therefore, Britain's civilised society directly contributed to complete corruption and collapse of some African countries where drug cartels corrupt vulnerable government by drug barons buying off local officials to pass their drugs via Africa. Hard drug sniff here and sniff there in Britain's media so British kids and Africans think to be famous you must be on hard drugs.

I am in a state of confusion about what civilisation or civilised society means living in Britain, if human behaviour does not count in classification of civilised society or just advances in making and use of modern science and technology items make a society to be called a civilised society. If coloured British-born or passport holder British parents are not among civilised British society, If white British criminals are not among British civilised society, 11,000 foreign prisoners in Britain prisons and 4000 white British in foreign prisons, are they among civilised British society? What is a civilised society? With present British alcohol abuse, drug culture, knifing, shooting, and killing, is Britain a civilised society? Can a society with confused behaviour people be called-civilised society? Can we have uncivilised people in a civilised society? I hope this is not the type of behaviour, Africa has been hoping to achieve. Alcohol culture has affected the whole British society, from royal family to homeless family in the street – a society that abuse alcohol, drug and nightclub. Do we have civilised society or civilised individuals? I think British civilised society is just about advancing in science and technology, without consideration on the society behaviour, weather good or bad. 'In the past 12 months in one local borough in Britain, they have had 5 murders, 33 rapes, 424 robberies and 2267 burglaries', what is civilised society then? I am thinking if I should go back to my country or stay in Britain and suffer depression because of thinking - most of Britain's mental clients are from ethnic minority. I was hoping after getting my British passport and finishing my postgraduate university courses I would feel like a human being in British society. I have no hope; I had no idea that Britain was not safe for my family and me. In Britain, at least 13 children are sent to the hospital because of alcohol related issues every day. British kids as young as 12 years old are made mentally ill by cannabis, Britain Health Service information shows that nearly 10,000 British teenagers are being treated for cannabis addiction and 45 per cent of 11 to 15 years old who are diagnosed with a mental disorder 'cannabis-related paranoia and schizophrenia' have previously smoked cannabis. Where are their civilised parents? I have not seen the civilised British society but have seen well-behaved Britons, civilised Britons. I realised I am in Britain for economic benefit with the behaviour I am seeing in London. So I will never give up staying in Britain since I am staying for economic benefit but I must go back to Nigeria-a rich country but with a poor society and hide my head in shame. Nigeria is the fourth largest production of crude oil but is faced with petroleum related problems cause by corrupt leaders. Yet the civilised society leaders still continue to support and encourage the corrupt Nigerian rulers, since majority of the embezzled money are banked in their countries and such money are taxed and used up by the western countries. Can the international criminal's western countries be Innocent to the confused economy and failed state of Nigeria? I can never trust some Britons then how can I call Britain a civilised society, as frightened members of the public, teachers, health workers and clergymen are buying body armour to protect themselves against Britain's growing epidemic of knife crime, should I go back home to

Nigeria or stay in Britain. In 1950th British society, my family as students had faced discrimination. In the year 2008, I am facing with other forms of discrimination and violence in Britain community, 'should my children stay in Britain, or should they go back to Africa.

Should I Stay?

Uncivilised issues in a civilised society, then what is civilised society? Bad behaviour has removed civilised from civilised society, should I stay or go? British unlock what your locked away, your good society behaviour. I thought British society should have been as good as a decent food. However, my future starts in Britain, tomorrow's science and technology items used today. In addition, some possible advantages of becoming a British citizen are very good, for example an African becoming British citizen gives full civic rights and duties in UK – the right to vote. If I becomes a British citizen ensures that I can never be deported from UK. Once I am a British citizen, I can take jobs which are only permitted to British citizens, for example, police officer or prison officer posts, and certain civil service positions. Also being a British citizen means that I no longer have to worry about the returning residents' rule – I can leave the UK for longer than two year and still be allowed back in. If I become a British citizen means that I become a European community national. This means that I should be able to work without restriction anywhere within the European community. In addition, once I am a British citizen I will be able to apply for a British passport. Sometimes a British passport is more useful for travelling to countries than Nigeria passport, for example, Britain is visa free to many countries. However, 'I am not a professor of sociology, I don't know much about society, civilisation or civilised society but I know what I like or dislike in a society. 'My story is full of horrifying tales of mistreatment but they are plenty of British people who care, support and respect themselves and what others deserve.' I have noticed that Britain has good roads, houses, rail system, free hospital system and treatments, good postal services, good social care and benefit system. 'If you are not working or disable the government pay for your house rent, give you free medical treatment and petty cash through state benefit for your food, clothing and basic housing living items – an opportunity which one could not get in any African society.' What make us have a home in a place is feeling safe and total comfortable in a society. However, a rich society is having community disability related issues and poor society is having community disability related issues. What is causing these problems? British people that look like angels in Nigeria do not look good in British society, despite living in one of the richest societies. Often it is hard to differentiate rotten men and women from good ones. The biggest single employer is the social security, claiming state benefit and about 70 percent of the population have no professional qualification but I have professional qualification certificate with no professional job. 'I have been to hell and back since I reach this civilised society, no good job after a university education but things seems to be well with me as I keep on moving in correct ways to survive.' However, I have a lot to gain if I live and work in Britain later in life than in Africa such as full right and privilege for my children free education and free healthcare and state benefit for my children and I, 'civilised society where everyone matters', and unrestricted movement across the European Union for business. The most important is that at aged, if I am not working, I can still have Britain state benefit like income support money and housing benefit money to pay my rent. 'The best things in life are free.' However, should I stay with the problems I am having at work place and bad events I am seeing in the community?

The New Year was just some hours old when the first teenager knife-murder of 2008 rocks Edmonton in the senseless knife crime blighting London streets – how many more this year? Edmonton I thought is one best place to live in London, an area I have lived for the past 10 years, it's just devastating news for Edmonton residents on the first day of the year - 2008. Many frightened teenagers say they carry a knife in case they are attacked. Despite the year first teenager's knife attack in Enfield borough, last year had 443 knife related crimes in Enfield, more than one knife crime in each given day. Just three weeks into New Year 2008 another person killed by knife and one wounded in the same Edmonton area of Enfield.

Home minister says London is not safe to walk at night.

Metropolitan police chief says London is a safe area. Police claiming that knife crime is falling.

North Middlesex University Hospital – accident and emergency section in Edmonton admitting more people suffering from stab wounds and are still in increase despite police claims that knife crime is falling.

Therefore, is it the policemen or hospital workers which of this group are civilised group and are telling the reality?

The police superintendent in-charge of Enfield borough operations admitted that Edmonton is a hot spot for knife crime but Enfield is still a safe place to live – the police officers must be joking.

How can a civilised society with a culture of carelessness be a safe place, God is with us. I am in a state of confusion about the British society. Civilised society teenagers needlessly stabbing people to death; it must be mentally related health issues and not because of poverty issues as the civilised society has a state benefit system. British youth-on-youth knife crime has swept the capital, London is increasing fear in the communities and I wonder what this generation will be in next twenty years. Britain streets now are rule by yobs not because the police have lost control, but because British government had a liberal apologist and penalty, 'we need death penalty for each shooting or stabbing to death.' A criminal released from prison is given decent accommodation and state benefit but not forced to start working, even when some of the released criminals are able to work, while innocent British that work cannot afford a decent accommodation. Most of the criminals released from prison ask their housing officer the amount of money the government will pay them for being in prison for years. Therefore, 'you commit crime, you go to prison and you get better housing and other state benefits in civilised society.' Let's be realistic about the fact that inner-city Britain today is not safe, I am scared to walk in London at night, I think that London police has lost the control on yobs. Should I stay in Britain or go back to Africa.

Why are British children killing each other in rich Britain civilised society? From my private dairy of 2007 - January to October, 52 youngsters have died by knife or gun, changes in attitude blamed as half all Briton's children live with just one parent and one in 20 girls in Britain gets pregnant before their 18th birthday. 'Teen single parents are fast becoming the lifestyle of choice for teen girls. Why? In just the middle of year 2008, more than 30 Britons have died by knife or gun. About 85 percent of killed youngsters from black community – maybe the white British society thought that they are black, so were uncivilised people in civilised society and then they behaved in uncivilised manner. No, they are British not uncivilised group, they have seen British employment discrimination, some Black British youngsters then thinking and with no hope of getting better jobs like their fellow white Britons after their university education then develop mentally related behaviour and end-up looking for fast ways of making money. Some civilised society black teenagers thinks that a human life is not worthwhile been poor, most of the kids just do not care if they live or die in crime battle for survival. Even American youngsters with gun culture have not killed each other like Britons or Arabs and North Nigerian societies with knife culture used knife badly to each other like British society. As the rate of knife-crime explodes on the streets of London, 'a boy of 10-years-old pupil robs a girl of 9-years-old with a blade.' What a senseless attack. British politicians are saying parents need to be educated on how to teach their children to behave well as violent crime increases in Britain's streets. I thought parents from civilised society are civilised before becoming parents on how to manage their children. What a confused society? British kids of 4-years-old could be forced to have sex and relationship education in primary school than wait until secondary school, claiming that any argument about starting sex education will put youngsters off rushing into sex - is this all what civilisation is about. British children as young as five commit crimes, including arrest for assault, drug offences, carrying a knife, fraud, arson, racial harassment and even sex offences. A survey of police force revealed. Should my children stay in Britain or go back to Africa.

What is civilised society with more British young girls becoming more pregnant and single mothers than those in developing country – uncivilised society behaviour in a civilised society? Are these young British women with three children from three different fathers, a civilised behaviour? Most of the children have no father, no family training, future stabbing and shooting generation, having children as to get high state benefit and support services like early Africans of 16th and 17th century having many children to help them in farming, a society in crisis. 'Young women having children from different men is becoming a civilised culture in civilised society, whatever you do in a civilised society is always new civilised life style.' What good have I learnt in this civilised Britain society of 21st century? With Britain's divorce rate is very high that there's no family in Britain that does not have one or two divorcers, from the royal family to the homeless person or family in the street. I hope this is not the right way to civilisation but just the right way to get more cash. Marriage is just a dream for many of Britain's youngest and poorest family. Where are the good old traditions British families' lifestyles I have come to see? I went to have a family in Britain without divorce so I can have English tea and talk about present British families' lifestyle issues. Is it possible of me having a family in UK without one of my children coping some of the UK bad lifestyles of alcohol or drugs dependency – should my children stay or should they go back to Africa?

I left my mobile phone in my working desk to use the project toilet room before I could come back to the office my mobile phone got missing. The four people in the office were all British and all refused to have seen the mobile phone I was using in their presence before I left to use toilet room and now I lost all my friends telephone numbers I stored in the mobile phone. What is wrong with people from civilised society?

I walked out of a train station from work at 23:00 pm hours and was speaking to my sister in America with my mobile phone as I walked home in south London. A fifteen-year old girl walked and passed in front me, showed me a knife and demanded for my mobile phone and I gave the phone to her and she ran away. I was shocked, scared and have never been so traumatised in my life. However, I was happy and lucky, she took my mobile phone but did not take my life away and I was terrified. Knifing-killing for phones in British civilised society of 21st century, I thought it's only in Nigeria-Lagos city we have many petty criminals as mentioned by the British high commissioner in Nigeria. 'Civilised society people may say that my story is so ludicrous.' Britons killing follow Britons because of mobile phone in 21st century – why?

A white co-worker in the same office once asked if I needed a cup of tea, I said yes, His reply was that 'I was enjoying expensive jokes. So when you reach Africa, you tell them that a white man made you a cup of tea, a white man is your office tea boy, 'tell your African people', showing his supremacy over me in the 21st century. I did not requested for a cup of tea but he asked if I wanted a cup of tea. 'We laughed together, a bit of laughter but I was having a little bit silly and abusive words from him.' In the 21st century British society, co-workers and even a university workers asking if we Africans still live on tree houses, if Africans have seen cement or brick houses before.

'No, Africans sleep rough on the streets like British street homeless people do, I said. But do you have road and streets; you mean you have bus in Africa one asks. No, we have no bus in Africa and we sleep rough in the bush pathway, but we use cows and camels for our public transportation I said.' 'Do we blame British education system for not taking good care of Africa study in the schools and colleges or consider the questions as racist issue. 'Workers behaving and looking like wild dominant bull Rhino in the offices – very territorial, very dangerous, and very powerful – I am sick of seeing every person in civilised society claiming to be superhero, should I stay or go home?' How can people in a civilised society claims they have not see/read about Africa society in the internet or newspapers – can Africans have one or two block building like our hostel in their society?

I am now a British-passport holder and had finished my university education in Britain but was not feeling like a British but an UNWANTED and UNWELCOME British. Is history repeating itself – discrimination openly seen in British society? Things are not as I had hoped, Britain has good internet, planed streets and roads, planed and big supermarkets, state benefits but, Britons behaviour have not been brilliant as we have been hoping in Africa society, openly white Britons are being promoted than their qualifications merited, discrimination in 21st century British society. I am taking on a string of low-paid jobs involving cleaning and night working, eventually started thinking and having stress and depression in my life. 'Should I stay and suffer depression, a mentally related issue or should I go back to Nigeria and bury my face in shame as my mates are now ahead of me?' Yet more people are risking their lives coming to Britain and other European countries via walking through the Africa Sahara desert, 'the world's largest hot sand desert and the world's second largest desert' to reach Europe, thousands are dying through waters to reach Europe. Why are my African-home people claiming that Europe is the best place to live? Why can't Europe send mass media to Africa and Asia informing them that living and maintenance in Europe society is not as easy as they think? Than claiming, all is goodness in Europe. I hope I am safe in Britain and Europe societies. The figures obtained under the freedom of information act showed there were 5,500 serious crimes involving knives in just three months in year-2007 in London area. Therefore, in each given hour, there is a knife crime in London, which shows the scale of the knife crisis blighting the streets of London. 'I think the figures would have been higher had all the other thousands of less serious offences including possession of a knife, events that do not cause injury and incidents that were not reported.' The figures include recorded 1,580 knifing, 26 murders, and 339 wounding and 1,134 muggings. This figure showed that seventeen people are stabbed or robbed at knifepoint in London every day higher than in Nigeria-Lagos city. I live in London city and the police have recorded crime figures of 906,885 in year 2006/07, which include burglary, gun crime, knife crime and domestic violence, racist crime, homophobic crime, robbery, violence against person, rape, motor vehicle crime and not all categories of crime had been on record and listed. Yet London is claiming to be a civilised society. Uncivilised events in civilised society, then what is civilised society? About 605 drug offences committed every day in Britain police reported. Even black people born in Britain tell their follow black people born in Africa, 'to F**k off and go back to your country, you monkey.' The comment used to be from white mentally disabled people in care or supported accommodation but not from them now, it is from a professional black British-born footballer. Why some black and white Britons who cannot read or write English language in 21st century, is this the British equality education standard we-Africans have be hoping to achieve? White and black Britain-born just speaking English that cannot be an achievement or make you to be a civilised person in English people's land, where is Britain's civilised society? Are these types of black British-born among the civilised British society? Black British-born telling Africa-born British to go back to Africa – claiming that they have funny accents. 'They may have funny accents but they speak, read, and write in Standard English language than most UK-born.' 'Looking suspicious to white Britons, black-born British because of my accent, I work/live with them in suspicious mind – should I stay or go home.'

I am working in hospital and hostel, with British hospitals a dangerous place, Europe worst infection rates, hospital super bug (MRSA) kills over 100 clients a month and disregard for basic hygiene blamed for worst case of killer hospital bug, faeces were found on bed rails and stairways in 2007 British society by health and safety inspection team. Human bodies are being left on British hospital wards over-night because of shortage of money to pay night porters to move bodies to a mortuary. I thought Britain is a rich and civilised country. 'I hope I will not carry the infection and later face health problem as I reach Nigeria.' I hope I am safe as over 1000 patients affected and 90 patients died in one hospital trust in Britain Kent and Sussex areas because of Clostridium difficile infection blamed on appalling hygiene standards and over 54,000 cases of Clostridium difficile infection in Britain.

Britain's health minister said, sorry for already died people.

Healthcare commission said, Litany of errors – we still have more errors. National Hospital Services: we have learned our lessons – still people are dying because of hospital infection diseases.

Kent Police may decide whether to bring charges on hospital boss for mismanagement – I am still waiting for the result of the police investigations.

'Uncivilised society problems in civilised society, what is civilised society then? It would have been world headlines news in media if this occurred in developing society, uncivilised society like Africa or Asia. 'Britain a civilised society that cannot clean or clear rubbish well, yet hospitals have cleaning companies that cannot clean.' Hope I am not suffering from any of the diseases and went home to African and died? A British doctor being investigated for death of 215 of his patients and forging most of his client's property to his gain has been jailed for life and however killed himself in the prison. 'I do not trust some doctors, so my organs are not for donation, and I know I will die but not dying halfway or being killed for my organs.' Should I stay or go home?

Why do ethnic minority and white British keep suspecting each other in a civilised society, living in the same area we are suspicious neighbours, working together in an organisation we are suspicious co-workers. Why should we continue coming and living together with suspecting mind? Why can the problem be resolved together with open mind? Britons why keep pretending that everything is fine, why can't we solve the problems or tell us it is over and it is time to stop coming over and go home? However, there must be something wrong for a society with 85 percent of it being white population to keep moaning about 15 percent of its population from ethnic minority group. 'I am from an uncivilised society hunting for civilised ways of behaving in a civilised society but ended up becoming a more uncivilised person.' In 21st century civilised society, you send an application for driving licence then a paid friend will do the practical test for you but you will be driving with the licence later. You send a job application form to any large organisation then a paid friend will attend the job interview for you but you will be working later, all the top staffs claiming that they do not know what is going on. It seems ludicrous when staffs makes a caricature about employment related issues in the offices in Britain's 21st century civilised society – another person complete a job application form, another person went for the interview for the same job and another person will be working for the same job position, why?

In employment, talent not privilege of being born in Britain, colour or years of being in establishment without qualification should count. Be paid and promoted based on how long you have worked in an organisation discourage workers to learn or seek for more education while working. However, where will university graduates start their employment with organisations if higher education is not valued – as an organisation cleaner? I thought Britain is one of the countries that encourage education in different parts of the world; why do you not value education any more. 'A criminal jailed for years cannot become a prison officer after release from prison. Can a well known criminal become a police officer after a lot of cases with the police? Can a patient in hospital become a nurse for be in hospital for years after treatment or a nurse becomes a medical doctor without training.' Some British workers should be ashamed, you do not have the experience or qualification, but you still want to be at the top position because of your family or friend connections.

Most of the jobs vacancies published in the British media has a sign that 'we do not discriminate but strives to maintain equal opportunities and welcomes all application from all members of the community regardless of their age, disability, gender/transgender, race/ethnicity, religion/belief, culture group or sexual orientation.' Yet all the jobs published have been arranged first who is going to take the jobs before it is being published in newspaper, wasting people time on filling application park of jobs that has already been given out by connection, jobs are published just to act as if the equal opportunity is been in practice in 21st century British society. 'I am still hanging my professional certificate in my room wall and waiting for a professional job.' Britain, a civilised society making policy and procedures that do not work – equal opportunity legislation. I do not blame the society since one of Britain's great fathers said 'in my own words says. 'What is wrong with British people (unfortunate British people-ethnic minority people) nowadays, why do they all seem to believe that they are qualified to do things far above their capabilities.' Sir, we are ready to work because we have British university education and training, and our certificate is for practice not just to be call a university graduate. 'I have been offered top jobs in housing in some other countries yet British housing organisations are going to the same country for qualified housing workers, does it mean Britain university education is not up to standard required by British government.' 'I am still confused why the colour of my skin, accent, and religion determines if I am a good worker or not.' Even I am having problem socialising in Britain as a Black British Christian with Black Muslim British. Should I go to my native home or stay in Britain?

In 21st century, British Muslim extremists openly call to kill anyone who is deemed to have insulted Islam in civilised British society instead of teaching unbelievers to believe in them. 'Hope I am safe in the 21st century British civilised society – should I go home or should I stay in Britain.' Some of the London bombers were bad Muslims, they drink, smoke cannabis a court informed, top Muslim religion centre officials told court, yet they fight in the name of Islam and was not stopped from visiting religion centres. 'Why are people killing in the name of God?' Can we have active and uncivilised Muslim among cultured and civilised Muslims in civilised British society? Are these British Muslim extremists among British civilised people or can there being uncivilised group in civilised British Muslim society. I am in frightening mood. What is civilised society?

A British Muslim teaching assistant who refused to remove her veil, burkha, niqab, burqa, or mask, name it what you like, during lessons with children, lost her claims for discrimination and harassment in Britain, going to court in one of the land birth of Christianity for Islamic veil, what a shame, she must be joking. Why in the British university Muslim women are in burkha? In the Britain Mosque guard in mask, In the British road Muslim ladies driving car in burkha, In the British supermarket Muslim women in mask, Even in government office Muslim women working in mask, it is call multicultural Britain society but the public says no to wearing veil, burkha, or mask in public area. 'Just what are the Muslim women hiding? They are claiming that the burkha is the thing that gives Muslim women the freedom to come out in public even in the 21st century Britain society.' I was happy in Pakistan and other Arab country I visited with their culture clothes seen everywhere and I will like to see western wears in Britain's society. 'Will Muslim countries allow western women to wear western clothes as they like in public area in Muslim society?' I am not racist and I have nothing against Muslims but the law must be equal for everyone in a civilised society. Some Muslim men refused cutting their beard and wear Islamic clothing but work in Britain's government offices, why not work in Britain's Islamic centres. 'Egypt's top cleric support Italy and France nations to ban full-face veils in schools and other public places. The cleric said the niqab dress was a custom of Saudi Arabia which has nothing to do with Islam.' Why, British Muslim claiming that full-face veils in public places are racist against Muslims. I think civilised and uncivilised societies are in conflict of different races, culture and interest. Is Islamic culture against western life style? Is Islamic culture the civilised life style? Is western culture the civilised life style? Is western culture against Islamic culture? What is civilisation? Is an uncivilised society because of views from different cultures? I will be happy seeing women covering their head hair for 24 hours in London in common simple styles for I have come to see European cultures not Arabian cultures in London city. I left fuming after my wife and I were banned from attending a Muslim wedding as a couple in London in 21st British society. I was send to the men room and my wife to the women room in England. 'Just like the 1940 to 1950 Europe and United States of America public bus transport system – separate bus for white people and another bus for black people.' Are we not in western society, can people practice ancient culture in a civilised society – traditional marriage. Is England not a civilised society? Why having different cultures in a civilised society? Where has England culture gone? A black British Muslim called me a pig and makes pig sound towards me for eating pig meat in Britain and I am a Christian in Britain – when did Britain becomes a Muslim nation? 'I am a pig for eating pig meat, one of the British best meats in Britain – why did he call me a pig in Britain nation?' Are we in Britain or Arabia Land? Should I prefer to eat Arabia food in Britain? 'A Muslim for visiting Mosques, wearing Muslim traditional clothes and using Muslim names however, living in a westerner lifestyle behaviour – having sex before marriage and drinking alcohol.' Is he a true Muslim? However, 'a taste for the native culture in foreign society is secret to beating depression.' I am a pig for eating pig meats in Britain – even some Christian group do not eat pig meat and they never call me a pig for eating pig meat. Why are some black Muslim that have being complaining about them being discriminated by white Britons are now discriminating to black Christian for eating white British food in Britain nation? My children facing sack from school after spoke of God in the classroom – let pray – is Britain not a Christian nation? Where are the Christianity ways of lifestyles I was told in African that I will gain a lot from it once I am in Britain? 'I thought Britain is a Christianity faith nation. Britain nation that destroy African society ancient gods are now a nation of different faiths, however when did Britain becomes a nation multi-faiths and a nation of multi-culture? I am missing English lifestyles in England the native home of English people and language. 'Black British Christian against black British Muslim and black British Muslim against black British Christian. White British against white British, black British against black British, white against black and black against white. What is wrong with civilisation with new uncivilised issues developing in civilised societies, should I stay in Britain or go back to my native African home? In addition, a Sikh Teenager, 14-year-old taken out of a north London school by his parents because he was banned from carrying a traditional dagger. Under Sikhism, the sheathed scimitar is one of five 'articles of faith' that must be carried at all times but local education authority chiefs and school governors disagreed that taking the five-inch blade into a school was a health risk. 'Why are human race, tradition lifestyle, religion, and civilisation in a complex relationship even in a civilised society?'

I work in a housing and support project with a person from ethnic minority but British-born and I am a British passport holder. Both of us work as housing officers. He is working with NVQ Level 2 in social care and I am working with NVQ Level 2 in social care and postgraduate degree in housing. He has 3 years working experience and I have 6 years working experience, yet he wants to be my manager because he feels and believes that he has more British in him (born in UK) than myself (British passport holder). He thinks that we-not born in Britain have come to Britain to take over their jobs, he told our white man manager. While I think that both of us are unfortunate British and does not know if we both are among civilised British society. If Britain is a civilised society, who are civilised Britons? Does being born in Britain make you a civilised person? Does being given Britain passport make you a civilised person? Does working and living in Britain make you a civilised person and Briton? Does your behaviour in Britain make you a civilised person? Does being white in colour make you a civilised person? What is the meaning of civilised person in the civilised British society? 'Does being born in Britain make you a civilised person? Why does having a British passport make you a civilised person?' Now the British ethnic minority person is the manager of our project and all the new five workers the project employed are from ethnic minority, from his father's native country. The new workers do not have required experience or qualifications, yet we have applications with required experience and qualifications but the British ethnic minority manager thinks that he needs some brothers around him. They cannot do the work well but the manager claims they are the best workers. The same manager 'Britain-born' from ethnic minority group complains about white discrimination on black, Asia and ethnic minorities is now discriminating against other groups. The manager claimed that it is equality and diversity in action by employing people from his father's original country because he is the only person from his country within our organisation. The manager also claims it is equal opportunity policy in action by taking his people that have been discriminated for long time as no other person from their native country except him works in our organisation. 'The policy and procedure made by government is now misinterpreted.' What is wrong with this civilised society? 'Is Britain moving from civilised to uncivilised society caused by a lot of black and ethnic minority people in Britain?' Eastern Europeans are responsible for 2310 crimes in the first six months of this year 2007? Their crimes activities have overtaken Jamaicans and Pakistanis' as the worst British offenders, Britain's foreign nationals are the worst offenders. You must be joking, so white Britons with 90 per cent of the Britain's population sit and watch them committing the crime; I think the white Britons are master planning the criminal activities. 'Did the white managers notice that I have more experience and professional qualification than him?'

I worked with a white British ex-homeless gambler in a hostel, he was employed under government programme, forcing homeless, reluctant and disruptive Britons to employment and training as to avoid depending on state benefit. As two of us were working on weekend shift and he thought, I was new in Britain and a black man than used the hostel petty cash £10 for his gambling life. He claimed later that I had taken £10 from the petty cash box. He was the key holder, the cash and key of the petty cash box was given to him during the shift handover meeting. Without knowing that I had been watching him going in and out of gambling house and he told a resident that he is going to play game. Later he told me that money is missing from hostel petty cash box and that I should pay half of the money £5.00 and he will pay £5.00 or he will stop me from working in the hostel. 'Yes, he did stop me from working in that hostel, as I was not called in that hostel anymore for work, a white British power, just in Britain.' I said no to his request of paying some money, he went to the residents and told them that I had put him in problem by taking £20 from project petty cash box. 'It is no more £10 but £20 he claims that belongs to the hostel and wants the residents to give him money.' My first experience of what a white British think of a black people and a newcomer. I did report him and was inform that his name will be removed from the organisation for some months until he had a rehabilitation process, he cannot work in vulnerable people's hostel anymore. I went to another hostel the same week and saw the same man working in a hostel owned by the same organisation and with promotion - key worker. He did not talk to me for more than two years I worked with him. Therefore, a black man is a criminal, first time I have been made a criminal in my life. Should I go or stay in Britain and suffer more depression?

I am a key worker to homeless residents and I fill job application form for the residents to work as hostel project workers. Now is my team leader, later my hostel manager – just for doing one or two day's course. I have finished my NVQ five years ago and university housing degree and I am still a project worker, he has not yet finished his NVQ level 2 or any university course. I have more experience and qualification than he does, yet I cannot get any promotion. He is getting promotion for being a white British and I am a black British. I am an unfortunate British now, 'why discrimination in vulnerable people care and support accommodation project? Why having confusion in crisis centre.' Now, the project introduces new council recycling service and the manager stops it because I was in charge asking if my native Africa has recycling system, if you like recycling service wait until you reach Africa he said to me. Should I stay or should I go?

I filled a job application form for another white Briton hostel resident, after two years of working in another hostel owned by the same organisation he was coming back to the same hostel to be my team leader. He has no professionally qualified training than two days course. I think the unskilled white

British workers are valued to money for the work they are doing and skilled black British workers are under-valued to money for their working, and that is why black people are not offered good jobs – they are overqualified. Equal opportunity, equalities bills and diversity policy are not set up for unqualified workers to fight the same job position with qualified professional workers, 'you have to have a qualified professional certificate to be a professional worker.' 'Why charity organisations that is fighting against people becoming vulnerable is now making people become vulnerable by not offering professional people jobs and promoting unskilled workers higher than professional qualified workers.' Should I go or should I keep staying in Britain with low in mood – thinking in each given day about family and my future?

I went to house manager post interview, four managers to interview me asked what I meant by mentioning qualified housing practitioner in my CV, if I was a medical doctor because I mentioned housing practitioner in my CV statement because they need a cheap doctor to work in their mental health hostels. I ask myself, 'I am now, an African man coming to teach English language to English people in England, English people's land.' I told the managers that I had two postgraduate degrees, one in housing, and another in social science, also NVQ level 2 certificate and nine years working experience in housing sector. I was asked to go home, that they will contact me, that I had a bright future, 'I was always being told that I had a bright future for the past five year during interviews.' So four white British managers each with NVQ level 3 certificate training and each with more than ten years working experience could not know what is a practitioner, still all the four manager claimed they are professional workers in housing with no professional qualification in housing, social work or health care as I learnt by chatting with them. I think the managers are trying to see my colour and check my month sound 'accent' as to know if I am UK-born or just British passport holder. It remains when they called themselves practitioner or professor without basic qualified qualifications because they work in professional sector.

I do not blame the managers as Britain prime minister said in my own words 'British jobs are for British (white) people. British minister said 'none UK-born passport holders are taking over major jobs in Britain claiming they are in UK for passport and job. British jobs are first for UK-born first, so officially we have three types of British people in UK – white British UK passport holders, coloured UK-born passport holders and foreigner born UK passport holders. Yet you are destroying my farmland and rivers in getting you crude oil and I have not said Nigerian crude oil sector are for Nigerian people. Yet Zimbabwe farmlands are for black Zimbabweans not for white Zimbabweans, why is British prime minister against Zimbabwean president for giving the black Zimbabweans their farmland since British jobs are for white Britons.

Why can't people in civilised British society get job without having to make connection like people in developing countries – uncivilised society. I have never gotten any job in Britain without having friends who works in that organisation or via church members helping with my application in 21st century British society, yet I am a qualified housing practitioner. Yet bunch of unqualified people are being given jobs, are been paid and are been promoted than qualified workers, my organisation called me to sign last year expenditure on my project which I was the manager, seeing over £35,000 that I have not yet spent but had recorded as spent. I then refused to sign but an ex-homeless manager signed for his project and my project as he was a manager also and claimed that he had signed for all the other projects whom their manager refused or are not available to sign, boasting that he has done it before and there was no problem. So within a short period of four years the ex-homeless manager has been promoted to higher position, a director that our organisation will be making use of, so he becomes the organisation's official fraudster worker as he can sign any form in his front. An ex-homeless manager becomes a director without much experience, no professional qualification while qualified and experienced managers still in their position as managers.

I have sent out about 500 housing job application forms and yet I am still looking for a housing job. Yet British housing organisations are still looking for housing professionals or practitioners to employ. Whom are they waiting to employ? 'Some friends or family members who are planning to do some housing courses or are studying housing course in the university.' If I used my African name and my qualifications in job application pack, I am not be short-listed for job interview, but when I use an English name and my qualifications, I will be called for job interview. Graduates should have a level but not at the bottom level of employment - a cleaner. After 5 years of postgraduate study in housing management, I am still a housing assistant worker not an officer, while my white mates at university are Area mangers or company directors, shows Britain's race discrepancy in employment. 'I think something is wrong with me and white Britons – my colour, discrimination in 21st century British society.' Is there any qualified ethnic minority worker who has not faced racist or discrimination at work in civilised British society of 21st century - unless you have some connections, or influence, to help you get ahead? Every worker from ethnic minority group has a story to tell. I speak at a rate that makes both white and ethnic British-born feel comfortable listening, general Standard English, they can hear and understand what I am saying but they want me to use British jargons, slang, or trendy UK languages. 'It is time I start teaching English people how to speak Standard English.' British employment sector in a mess why? Race, discrimination, and equal opportunity policies just on paper but not in practices like 'English person writing, reading and speaking English that should not be achievement in England.' Policies meant to give access to the right people are now against the right people – the trained and qualified people caused by organisation human resource team. When you have qualified certificate to work, organisation human resource team will tell you, we need experienced people. When you have the experience, organisation human resource team will tell you, we need trained and qualified people. When you tell organisation human resource team that you have experience, training and qualification then it is time to check for your colour and accent not you qualifications or skills. A housing human resource manager without professionally qualified housing qualification cannot accurately define the difference between house, homelessness, and home. I was in a project when a resident was admitted into a hostel, 'within some weeks we noticed that he is drug dependent and have committed two crime involving police within the weeks he stayed in the hostel. He befriended the project manager because she used drug and with a period of six years he has been promoted to project worker, team manager, hostel manger and director for just doing two days course, while qualified professional workers - his key workers are still project workers, an act in 21st century British society.' Where are our organisation's human resource team, is the equal opportunity policy working, I am seeing discrimination openly in 21st century British society. It is ridiculous and why has bureaucracy gone mad in a civilised society? What a shame. I thought you have to be professional qualified to have a professional job – for a person to practice as a medical doctor you have to study medicine. 'Sometimes I keep looking as mistake repeat itself often and on at work site. The gap between some of the manager's ability, our expectation and desire, and daily experience at site proved too frustrating to bear but I have nothing to go home for or stop working – what about paying my bills?'

I have never seen managers and consultants coming to manage me who has more experience and qualification than I do. I will be happy to get managers or directors with more experience and qualifications to manage me, my moral and hope will improve that I will be in that position in future and will learn a lot from my line manager; it seems all jobs post in Britain are political appointment even in charity organisations. I asked my white British woman manager, how she managed to get a job in my project after she has seen my experience, training, and qualification was surprised and she looked at me as if I was a movie in TV. Her answer was that her husband works in a council in North London, helps our organisation in their contract and was given work in our organisation, in favour of her husband's support in giving contracts to the organisation in 21st century Britain's civilised society. She has not worked in housing organisation before, has no qualification in housing, and has no management qualification or managing experience and the post is not a political appointment. Her new deputy manager is a worker from ethnic minority group but has no professional qualification 'still many unanswered questions about taking unprofessional workers in professional sector and them being promoted more than qualified workers.' Later our area manager asked me to assist her in the project in case she needs help and I left the organisation when I notice that she is about to start a course I had finish five years ago and yet I was not promoted. 'I thought the most qualified and experienced worker take the top job in civilised society.' I thought that Britain's bank crisis of 2009 would have taught Britain organisations to stop discrimination at work places – none of the British heading bank directors has professional qualification in banking in a civilised society. 'Professional working site without professional qualified workers – chief executives without professional qualification, directors without professional qualification, area managers without professional qualification, site managers without professional qualification, and frontline workers without professional qualification but all claim to be professional workers for working in professional sites via connection – where has the university trained professionals and practitioners gone?' I am still hanging my university certificate in my flat wall.

I once asked my housing consultant a question and he told me housing is not his field of training. I started thinking what he will then be doing with his housing consultant position because I am a qualified housing practitioner and did send an application for the same job but was not even short-listed or called for interview. He is doing a job he has no training, experience or qualification on while a person who have the required qualification and applied for this job has no job. I thought Britain valued quality education and am in a well-educated society. 'Britain don't moan, act against discrimination, most qualified get the top job, a train nurse for nursing post not as a care assistant worker, a graduate of housing study for housing office not as support housing assistant, I do not value the positions-manager, consultant, area manager, or director in British society anymore.' What I always asked anybody who mentioned above jobs position is, are you more qualified to be in that position than other workers and what is your experience and qualifications to be in that post. 'Is it time to stop feeling guilty about discrimination in a civilised society? Let talent and not ethnic origin or colour decide, civilised society downplaying the importance of education.' The education I have wasted a lot of time and money on.

Should I stay in Britain or go back to Nigeria, in the last three years, 21 premiership footballers' homes have been burgled in the north-west of England, often while the players were at a match. The robberies are calling match away-day unwanted visitors by security team. My house may be the next to visit while I am at work. I will call them office working-day robberies. 'Funny names for criminal activities, Proof, crimes are funny in a civilised society.'

It is not easy to leave your native home society and base in another society as a home, what the early Europeans suffered before reaching African and Asian society. I am not in Europe by chance; it took a lot effect before I reached London. My challenge is how to make myself and other ethnic minority group relevant to the next generation white Britons as to avoid popular history 'discrimination' events repeating again. However, with crime 'linked to learning difficulties', which probation officers fear will increase re-offending rates according to a study. Do we now blame nature, mental illness, parents, security forces, or God for yobs culture and bed behaviour in civilised society? 'Drinking alcohol is prohibited in any public transportation system – yet you see people drinking alcohol in public buses and trains. Why money doesn't buy you happiness in civilised and rich society? Parents let catch up with family and society decent living in a civilised society by advising our children. Parent's advice, the art of children luxury living at home for less, then we enjoy stylish society living. Now, facing up to the challenges of being poor in a rich society when I becomes aged, without fair pension, if I have the misfortune to be one of the addict parent in the street, my children suffer as they fight for a better life. 'Society where drugs rule our future generation-children suffer.' A boy-16-years old living in my hostel said, 'seeing my family condition, sometime children need to take risk for better future living.' Parents children life your say, you are the shape of children future, plan your aged life and advice your children for a brighter future for all. The high rate of parental substance misuse – heroin, cocaine, marijuana, methamphetamine, and many are also drinking heavily is a cause for concern for child protection practitioners and decent parent with children in civilised society. 'Parents de-fuse the society problem with good lifestyle; parental substance misuse is not something to laugh about in a civilised society.' Our society future is in our hand. However, how bright does my children future look in 20 years time in the British society, not good, should we stay in Britain or go back to

Africa. However, living in Britain is hard but I have no choice.

Civilised People
Behaving Badly

Who is afraid of big bad news of civilisation –
civilised society with uncivilised issues? Ancient
events are alive and thriving alongside modern
society – then what is civilised society? I have
been in Britain and Seeing is believing, I think the
rats - corruption and greed in developing nations-
uncivilised society are also in developed nations
- civilised British castle's, government houses and
general British society, may be in form of mice
– discriminating and cunning. I am in Britain, a
rich and civilised society, I think civilisation is all
about the society that made use of modern science
and technology items first, the electric items I am
now using and are widely used in Britain, will be
widely used in uncivilised society in coming years.
I have known what civilised society is all about,
'civilisation is the ability to act in good manner

but not tell the truth, however, not causing any problem while managing your ways to get what you want.' I have not learnt any good behaviour in this civilised society. Not as we-Africans think and hope, as there's nothing good to write home about Britain's civilised society behaviour in 21st century, with the below latest sickening example of yobs culture rule and general British bad behaviour. Civilised Europeans which look, talk, and behave like angels in Africa for instance in Nigeria. Why are people in the civilised societies acting as if they are superior and acting like supercharger item to the other part developing world? However, here is their true behaviour in British society and it is shocking and disbelieving in 21st century for Africans – 'a catalogue of errors and crime issues that shames the British people and other civilised societies.'

'In Britain, over 3,000 counterfeit DVDs, including a hoard of vile porn have been seized in a raid on a London Hackney home by British police and federation against copyright theft – counterfeit in Britain's civilised society of 21st century.'

'A British 49-years-old police officer and a married man charged with possessing more than 2,000 indecent images of children and 15 counts of making the images. I thought British police officers are angels.'

'A British mother gets £130,000 in benefits by falsely claiming her healthy son was sick and putting him through medical hell for six years. The healthy boy had to have an unnecessary operation, was forced into a wheelchair, spent his young life seeing doctors, was put on needless special diets and feed pump. The evil mum gets £20,000 a year in disability allowances and a car by claiming for his illnesses over six-and-a-half years.'

'A young British father 23-years-old stabbed repeatedly to death on dance floor in front of hundreds of horrified clubbers. Another British mother 22-years-old left her two years old son home alone to spend a weekend partying all night; she left some food in rubbish bin liner in her flat kitchen for the two-years-old to scavenge for food when he woke-up.'

'A 14 years old British white boy stabbed to death in north London area last night only for his phone mobile. A British killed by a British just because of mobile phone in 21st century British civilised society. What a senseless attack.'

'A British banker was jailed for seven-and-a-half years after admitting five counts of conspiracy to supply class-A drugs and one of being concerned in supply of drug. He made thousands of pounds selling cocaine from his office desk - fund a playboy lifestyle by setting up drug deals on his office phone. He was caught by police, who recorded his phone line calls. Even British bankers are in drug selling deal.'

'Two white British drug addict brothers 26 and 25-year-old jailed for life for killing a hard working father 54-years-old, who stood in front of his getaway car to stop them from stealing his £5 van radio but they ran over him. Britons killing follow Briton for just £5 car radio. Where is the British civilised society?'

'London night bus driver and passengers living in fear over gangs like Nigeria - Lagos city. A driver faced being sprayed with CS gas, simply because he asked passengers-group of young males to pay a bus fare or show a travel card. Last year, 134 drivers was assaulted and the passengers threatening to be robbed by young gang, the problem is spiralling out of control – what should I write home about Britain's civilised society.'

'In front of frightened schoolchildren and their shocked parents, a 65-years-old lollipop man was beaten with his stick and repeatedly kicked, as he lay defenceless on the floor with head injuries, after the lollipop man told a driver not to park on yellow lines in front of a school. The council boss and police are disgusted and called it a deplorable attack. A lollipop is an older person volunteering his services to ensure children cross road safely to school. What is the civilised society all about?'

'Five men convicted over Britain's biggest cash depot stealing, the gang were able to make off with £53 million, after the gang did not have room for more cash in their van and left behind £21 million, £32 million of loot is still at large. Some of the gang members were workers in the cash depot.

Men from civilised society stealing, what is wrong with British bankers.'

'A male nurse 34 years old raped a girl of 16-years-old in accident and emergency hospital toilet room in oxford after the girl took an overdose – a court heard. The male nurse notice the girl was feeling drowsy and wobbly after treatment and the male nurse claiming he need her urine sample, take and force her to a disabled lavatory, she fell over and he closed the toilet room and raped her on the floor. After the sex attack, he apologised, got her a fresh gown, and helped her back to her cubicle. The nurse admits sexual activity with a child under 18 years old, by a person in a position of his trust or responsibility – the nurse said he is ashamed for having sex with youngster but denies rape. A nurse in 21st century Britain's civilised society's act.'

'A granddad 95-years-old, partially–blind and walk with stick died after confronting a gang of thugs, so we have criminals in civilised British society, a civilised society area not safe even for poor old man of 95-years-old, It is disgusting.'

'British mother of two teenage children, 34-years-old filmed having sex with boy 13-years-old was jailed for 15 months after admitting twice having intercourse with the youngster at her home. What is wrong with these civilised society women?'

'An elderly white British couple 83 and 84 years old and their son 47 years old made fake Egyptian and Greek antiques in their garden shed and conned art galleries and museums all over the world-Vienna, London, New York etc of more than £5 million, the couple given months suspended and son given four years and eight months jail. Therefore, White British family involving themselves in faking items – British Fakers.'

'More than 900,000 British use and buy cocaine – Britain is Europe's biggest cocaine users. Is this what a civilised society is all about Britons?'

'Two white Britons sex beasts 21 and 19 years old jailed for sickening attack that drove a young mum to kill herself. The white lady 22 years old was unconscious when she was assaulted in front of her sons, aged four and 21 months by one gang while another gang boys filmed it on his mobile having sex with her. She late took an overdose of pills that killed her, after police identified her in the film circling in the city and showed her the film having sex with two boys and her children saying don't do that to my mum. Uncivilised act that you can never see in uncivilised society of Africa and Asia is in British civilised society.' Uncivilised act you can see in uncivilised society in civilised society, then what is civilised society?

'A British Reverend, a father of two has more than 600 child pornography images on his computer. The vicar was getting a barrister to support him after Church of England mentioned that the church are upset and not the standard that they expect from the church clergy and will end the vicar's contract and work with the church of England. Is pornography civilised or uncivilised behaviour in a civilised society?'

'Five Muslim doctors who live and work in Britain among the car bomb plot in Britain, I thought medical Doctor's are civilised individual or group and being in Britain a civilised society at least will make you to be a civilised human being. A British medical Doctor killed people and himself. Who are the civilised group?'

'A white British man 57 years old 'canoeist' comes back from the dead after five years apparently drowning in a canoeing accident and has been arrested on suspicion of fraud. Lifeboat crews spent 85 hours at sea, which involved searching 200 square miles around the incident site for several days in March 2002 and cost an estimated £70,000. Even a death certificate was issued after an inquest recorded an open verdict, allowing his wife to claim on his insurance. He lived inside the same room with his wife in his house for five years and his wife force pretending that he was dead. British media and police call him a canoeist but I call him my teacher – yes, he taught me not to trust some Britons even with his wife not reporting him. Britain do not force pretend, a white Briton family acting this way, I thought a Briton with family behaves better. He faked his death with his family because of loan and debt he owns, went missing, presumed died after his wrecked canoe was found in the seaside. My teacher-canoeist also faked the passport he used to move to Panama City. 'Therefore, Britons family can be engaging in faking international passport business.' The canoeist comes back from death to take revenge on his wife 54-years-old for money transfers totalling more than £650,000 to Panama city, his insurance and death benefit cash claimed by his wife, selling of their houses and runaway on reaching my teacher-canoeist at Panama city to join him after furious row. The canoeist believed the only way to bring his wife down and get some of the money-cash she ran away with, is to be alive again, he walk into a police station claiming he was confused, thus he indirectly reporting his wife. His wife 'Britain mother of all liars' was now facing jail with the husband for force pretending and obtaining money by deception, obtaining property by deception and lying about her husband death. What a shameful act, the canoeist's death comes to be outright lies; I thought British families are angels. What good behaviour have I learnt in this civilised society?'

'British broadcasting corporation services Boss under fire and GMTV was fined £2 million after cheating viewers out of more than £20 million. BBC confessed to a further string of incident where viewers were deceived in Antiques series flogs it and faked winner of blue peter competition. Where is the BBC's reputation for honesty and integrity in faking winners, I think the British society is moving from civilised to uncivilised society. I am starting to lose interest in what I see and hear from the British media, just saying it is white colour crime but very soon, I hope it will be black colour crime. 'I do call and pay money during the programme, where do you keep my money?'

'Killer Asian grandmother, 70-years-old, who masterminded the honour killing of her daughter-in-law through arranging for her brother to strangle the woman and throw her corpse into a river as they visit India for a family wedding was jailed for life. The victim's husband also jailed for life for taking part in planning the killing of his wife. Her body was not found. She was killed for been westernised and wanting a divorce. Killed for been westernised in British society, is Britain an uncivilised society? Is this Asian Briton or Asian in Britain among the British civilised society?'

'A British comedian 58 years old took the virginity of a 14 years old girl during an acting lesson. He had sex with her in his dressing room, his car and his home, should a dad from a civilised society behaved in this way. Behaving like African sugar daddy, old men having sex with teenage girls, just for the girls to get money to pay their school fees and buy school uniforms. Why do we have uncivilised Africa's sugar daddy lifestyle in British civilised society?'

'A caretaker found a bag of British royal mail dumped in his estate as rubbish and other bundles of mail were dumped in a skip in another estate. Royal mail has launched an investigation as some of the mails contained bills, private letters and gifts and some mails opened. Letters posting problem in civilised British society. Postmaster, please mind the letter with my payslip with sign – PRIVATE & CONFIDENTIAL.'

'A British Asian girl 23 years old killed another Asian pregnant love rival 17 years old after having an affair with her husband. She stabbed her 43 times with a 17 cm kitchen knife and was jailed for more than 13 years. I thought Britain has police and social welfare services department. Why are this British Asians behaving like they are in Asian villages?'

'Three Britons who kept a man with learning disability like a dog in a shed was given 10 years jail term each. The man with disability was imprisoned after he accidentally damaged a friend's car. The disabled man was repeatedly beaten, burned and humiliated until he died after a month. The three white Britons videoed the man with disability and kept a diary in which they recorded his punishments. Behaviour of whites in civilised British society, Where are the civilised society then?'

'Five gang of British drunk teenagers, three aged 17, one-aged 16 and another 19-years-old vandals murdered 47-years-old, a father-of-three by kicking his head like a football in the street as his family watched on hopelessly. The teenager gang admitted to drinking up to ten cans of cheap lager beers each earlier that night. The 47-years-old father was killed as he went to the gang and complained of them making life miserable for his family and neighbours as the teenagers vandalise vehicles in his street.'

'A British woman was caught smuggling cocaine from Peru and admitted she knew the risk but needed money. She was allegedly promised £5,000 for delivering nearly 4 kg of the illicit drug to a British address, 'I am unemployed and £5,000 is a lot of money' said the British woman. In Africa, Europeans walk pass our airport counter without being searched because we thought they were angels. Now I know you do not deserve that respect, Europeans are also drug dealers too.'

'A former British councillor has being jailed Four months for setting up a spy camera to film women and teenage girls as they use his bathroom, a British councillor in a sex act. What a shameless act.'

'A British city lawyer was killed by 2 teenage thugs, the killers stabbed him twice in the chest, slashed his face and cut his arm and the lawyer eventually handed over his possessions telling them – 'you have got everything, can I go now but they killed him just for his mobile phone' in 21st century civilised British society. Britons are killing a fellow Briton lawyer to get his mobile phone.'

'A British man carrying a large butcher's knife burst into a co-operative shop. He threatened staffs while stealing cigarettes and cash from the till before escaping in 21st century British society. Why kill because of cigarettes in Britain's society.'

'Three Briton yobs spat in the face of a Muslim woman in a burqa as she travelled home from a memorial ceremony for the victims of the July 7 bombing, calling her a terrorist and subjected her to barrages of racist abuses in front of her four children, aged 4 to 11. I thought that people from civilised society should involve the police than taking the law into their hand.'

'A British lady who searched for vulnerable 12 and 13 years old girls, take them away from their home, lured them into prostitution and rewarded them with cracked cocaine and designer clothes has been arrested. So there's teenage prostitution in civilised British society.'

'A British man was jailed for lifting, battering and kicking a drinking partner to death for stealing his can of beer. He used a rounder bat to fell the drunken partner on the doorstep of his home and repeatedly kicked him on the head until he died. Killing because of a can of beer in Britain's civilised society in 21st century. What is civilised society then?'

'A British church vicar sent a-naked-man birthday card to a married woman he was having sexual relationship with, the priest caused the marriage to break. I thought Christianity is a way to civilisation, what God has joined together let no man separate. It's just British vicars who can separate what God has joined together.'

'Naked sex pictures of Britons in international newspapers, British's vile sex on Cyprus love boat. Shock pictures of boozed-up young British girls performing oral sex on naked strangers for money, British girls were ordered to kneel and stimulate oral sex with peeled banana fruits. 'British young girls put on the stage and get to stimulate sex with boys from the audience, young British couples having sex openly in the shipyard – a ship of shame.' Is all this part of civilisation? However, once they are killed, then Britain's society and their parents come to claim they were angels. Angels of selling sex to the public, another form of prostitution in 21st century in Britain's civilised society.'

'A British Muslim boy killed his sister for falling in love with the wrong man, a non-Muslim. British government is considering outlawing forced marriage to help stop honour killings but drew back, over fears that it may backfire. British Muslim parents forcing their children on arranged marriage in British society of 21st century. Is British Muslim not among the British civilised society and why have a different law for Muslim marriages in Britain?

British detectives review 117 honour killings cases in civilised British society of 21st century. Britain has not yet managed their internal honour killings and they are advising other country on how to manage their honour-killing problems.'

'A British father drugged and suffocated his daughter with chloroform in revenge for his wife's affair, a court heard. In addition, a British businessperson strangled his wife then buried her in the spot where he had sex with his prostitute lover weeks before, a jury heard. Do we have only civilised individuals and not civilised society? Where is the civilised society?'

'A British prison officer 31 years old, a mum-of-three got pregnant in a gymnasium cupboard in the prison by international drug smuggler 38-years-old, who is doing 22-years at prison. He then arranged cash packages via his agents to the prison officer after her pregnancy, a court heard. The prison officer sends mobile phone and top-up vouchers to the drug dealer in prison so they could keep in touch. The officer confessed that the drug dealer gave her money and the £14, 330 found under her parent's bed on police raid. The prison officer pleaded guilty to misconduct in public office and was jailed for nine months and family were given suspended sentence for admitting aiding and abetting. The baby will be born while she was in jail, a jail prison officer having a baby in a prison yard; I call the new baby 'an executive prison baby.' 'A worker in a civilised society in a culture of carelessness – a prison officer jailed and becomes a prisoner, why.' British family knowingly taking money from a well known criminal, where is Britain's civilised society?'

'A white British father stabbed his son of four to death and knifed his teenage daughter at his home and then went to pub to drink alcohol – Britain a nation of alcohol abuse culture.'

'63 years' old British catholic priest has admitted having sex with a student who died and her body was seen under his chapel floor. In the same church, the church caretaker accepted having sex with the same student the same period the catholic priest was having sex with her and later killed her. The church caretaker was jailed for killing the student and two other bodies of missing teenagers, 15 and 18-years-old found in the former house of the church caretaker. So the catholic priest and church caretaker had sex with the same girl in the chapel, prostitution in the church chapel.'

'A British man 38 years old, a father of two, strangled his cheating wife, 32 years old in their bed and had sex with her dead body as to be the last person to have sex with her. To show he loved her, he lay on the top of her died cheating wife body until he ejaculated. The cheating wife gave her husband 'house-husband' £40,000 to leave and go for another wife, after she had an affair with ex-boyfriend and discovered they still had feelings for each other but her husband refused leaving her. Nothing good have I learnt in this British civilised society of 21st century.'

'Britain female tennis coach, 29-years-old forced and seduced a girl 13-years-old into lesbian affair-sex. The youngster insisted that for 14 months, she was forced to have sex with her but she never wanted to do any of it. The coach told the little girl that she would get her thrown out of the prestigious academy if she told anyone about the sex act. Later the mother of the little girl found her young child involving in a sex act in a bed with her coach. She was jailed after she was convicted of molesting her student. An uncivilised event I have never heard in an uncivilised society is now in a civilised society. Britain must be the origin of all the modern uncivilised events in Africa.'

'A white British fraudster woman 65-years-old jailed for five years for a £2.4 millions benefit fraud she ran from a secret room behind her bedroom wardrobe, her mute cousin 63-years-old was jailed for four years for running a highly organised fraud. The two Britons hijacked nearly 200 identities and used some of them to apply for state handout ranging from council tax benefit to income support.'

'A drug dealer 26-years-old in London Palmers Green area was jailed for nine years for drug dealing and money laundry. During a raid, officers found boundless of cash in a wash machine, the hallway, the dustbin, various cabinets and more than £24,000 under the bed. The 26-years-old was also guilty of trying to launder money that he made from selling the drugs. A civilised white Briton man selling drugs, we must be in a confused society.'

'A British married teacher 29 years old has admitted loving and having sex with a boy of 16-years-old from her classroom. The boy told court that he had sex with her at a hotel and at home while her husband was at work, that they had sex two to three times in each given week.'

'Some of the British love, sex and killing acts– a jealous husband who tapped his estranged wife's email and mobile phone, before stabbing her to death was jailed for life. Another husband faces life in jail after being convicted of murdering his wife, whose body has never been found – he fed his wife body to the pigs. In addition, 'Lovejoy' kills his wife over seven lovers. Again, Milkman murdered ex and mate before killing himself. The above actions in Britain's civilised society and what is a civilised society then?' Male British social worker sacked and jailed for having sex with his client, a woman he was treating for post-natal depression. In addition, a police officer subjected a girl to ten years of systematic sexual abuse, court heard. Moreover, a married Church of England vicar has quit his post following an affair with milkman's wife, a relationship which started when the woman worked as his church curate. Another 54-years-old British nurse groomed his eating disordered and vulnerable women patients for sex. He had sex with at least 20 of his patients. Acts of developing countries in a developed country – what is more shameless.'

'A British matron of dishonour stole £100,000 from her sick and dying clients in hospital bed and used the stolen money for five star holidays in Switzerland, Italy and France, court heard.'

'A British wife who married her second husband bigamously killed him on his 31st birthday by food poison. It was only hours after her husband's death from an overdose of aspirin and the anti-dispersant dethiepin; she was waiting to be sent to trial for fraud, as she was trying to get hold of his £35,000 death benefit. She killed her husband because she feared her double life was about to be exposed.'

'A Nigerian international gang that stole more than 120 Mercedes cars a month faces jail. The gang operation systematically targeted older models of the car for their part, which were exported to Nigeria in a business worth more than £70,000 a month. This Nigerians hold British passports, are this Nigerians are among the civilised British society or uncivilised Nigerians in a civilised British society.'

'One in 10 British is a shoplifter; they nicked £1.7 billion worth of goods. Londoners are most likely to buy stolen goods with 32 percent of adult admitting they will buy stolen goods. About 3.7 million British aging from 16 to 65 years are shoplifters. I am just learning bad things than good behaviour in a civilised society.'

'Four British boys who filmed themselves raping a teenager on their mobile phones were given lengthy jail teams; they threatened their 17 years-old victim with a knife. I thought sex should be private matter or is group sexing the modern civilised way of having sex.'

'A White British bank manager stole from his bank more than £20 million, set up 70 accounts to launder the money and 57 separate cash withdrawals in the weeks before being caught and jailed for 10 years. Even white men can be cunning-thief.'

'A National Health Service Doctor conned out more than £40,000 in wages by forging time sheets for shifts she never worked, a court heard. Even doctors in civilised society forge, why?'

'Two corrupt British police officers who leaked information about inquiries including two murder cases have been jailed. They leaked information and they got designer suits in return – just like in African and Asian uncivilised society.'

'A British Ugandan Birmingham council finance manager who stole more than £1 million to buy five houses and a luxury car was jailed for seven and half years. Should this Ugandan be called a civilised Briton or be called a man from a developing country but lives in Britain.'

'British priest jailed for helping paedophile groom girl for sex. A Reverend father, who gives more than £20,000 to friends to fund the grooming of a girl for sex was jail for 5 years.

Another male British priest who molested children got 5 years jail term. He used his trusted position as a vicar to molest children in his parish. The priest sexually abused six boys age 12 to 16 years old. A respected British priest in man to little boy sex act why? What a shame.'

'A British police officer 31 –years- old is facing jail after being convicted of masturbating next to a female suspect in a squad car and also trying to force his hand into the thong of the 25-years-old female victim. A Behaviour of a police officer in civilised British society of 21st century.'

'Some of the British Teachers great acts - A male teacher began a four years and three months prison sentence after an affair with his pupil before he was 15 and had sex with him at least seven times. The teacher took the teenage boy's virginity and sexed in a school stock cupboard three times, twice in the school male toilets and on two other occasions in a park. A male teacher having sex with male pupil in British society – we have not seen such a behaviour in African society.

Another teacher, who sent pornographic Christmas card to pupil as young as 14 years, was jailed for 14 months.

In addition, dream teacher sobbed in court as she told court how a pupil forced her to perform a sex act on him, the sex act was filmed and also had sex in a car.

Another teacher, who sent pornographic Christmas card to pupil as young as 14 years, was jailed for 14 months.'

'Britain's youngest mother-to-be at 11-years-old is eight months pregnant; smoking cigarette and her family house inside is a slum. Her mother lives on state benefit and a drug user - heroin. Her mother is 34-year-old and a single mum to six children by three different dads, boasting that she's not angry with her daughter but proud of her. What is wrong with this civilised society, '11-years-old child having a baby, a baby having a baby' I am just in a confused mood. In addition, British boy at 21-years-old has seven kids by seven women in seven years, does not pay any money for brood-children and lives on state benefit and family also lives on state benefit. He refused to wear condom and had his first child at 15 – so an African man with many wives in the year 1920-40 had come from a civilised society before the European arrived and mismanage their society. 'Seven-seven-seven dad, you are a confused civilised human being. Also in Britain – one man with 5 wives and 17 kids and the 49 years old says he is a lucky man. Another white British serial bride conned lonely hearts men by making them believed she was suffering from a terminal breast cancer and did not want to die before she married. She married more than six men and got gifts including diamond engagement ring, using their credit cards, holidays, seduced them and then stole their cash and promise them of sex, her crime spree may have netted £250,000. She admitted deception in crown court and sentence. Why a Briton in fake and bogus wedding just to get money? In addition, a professional British woman of 44-years-old mother of three grown-up sons has born twins and abandoned them in a car park. The woman, who had become pregnant during an affair with an old school friend, gave birth in the bathroom at home while her husband was away working. She then wrapped the twins in blankets and put them in a supermarket cardboard box, which she left outside the hospital's maternity unit when they were just six hours old. Another incident, a cheating girlfriend had a brief affair with a man she met at work. She gave birth alone at her home and she wrapped the stillborn baby in a carrier bag with some bin bags and hid it in the boot of her car after keeping her pregnancy a secret from her partner and claiming that she was putting on weight. In civilised Britain, we are having bigamy, bigamist and child killing. Where are the good traditional British family systems I have come to see? 'A civilised society behaving in an uncivilised manner, what is civilised society then?'

'A deputy head teacher 48 years old who had sex with two teenage pupils 15 and 13 years has been jailed for five years and three months. The relationship developed after the girls confided in their deputy teacher that they were thinking about having sex with a boy and the teacher offered to meet them to show them how to have sex. Staffs, who supposed to support people, are now misusing their positions.'

'A British unmarried priestess quits Church of England and top church job after becoming pregnant. She believes in having children without marriage. She was force to leave her job by the church authority. I thought God welcomes and likes children.'

'A British foster mother, a devoted Jehovah's witness routinely beat, abuse and starve three youngsters in her care, forced sticks down their throat and made them eat their own vomit and rat excrete, a sicken abuse for 19 years' was jailed for years.'

'A British nurse who tried to kill an elderly widow with a drug overdose hoping to inherit £10,000 was jailed for 10 years.'

'Five British gang of bully have made a man with severe learning difficulties eat 70 paracetamol tablets and marched him to a viaduct (100 ft) 35 meters, where he fell to his death, a court heard. A British men, subjecting a human being to bully, humiliation, violence and physical abuse to death in 21st century. What is civilised society then?'

'22 British passport officers were arrested over faked UK passports. Over 10,000 UK passport applicants are faked and even the man who plotted to use a radioactive 'dirty bomb' in London was issued nine passports.'

'A White British gang flooded streets with £14 million faked notes; the British gang printed millions in fake £20 notes at 85 years old granny's flat. The three generation of the same family produced so many fake £20 notes that the whole banking system was under threat, a court heard. Britons in faking of British pound notes, are they joking? White Britons fakers are criminals in the 21st century British civilised society.'

'£150,000 worth of fake England shirts was seized in raids by British officers in Britain. A major counterfeit ring was exposed after a raid on a secret factory crammed to the ceiling with fake clothing worth around £1.5 million to rogue British dealers. The gang use Olympics logo to rip off internet users.'

'British immigration chief facing a sex charge for visa probe, the 53 years officer from Ghana was offering refugee teenage girl from Africa help in return for sex and brought shame to the British home office. African disease (sugar daddy), old Africa men having sex with young teenage girls and in return give the girls money for school fees or support for work is now in Britain. Government officer's offer help in return for sex favour, a classic example of third world abuse of power in Britain's civilised society in 21st century. What a shame.

Also senior British home office worker from Zimbabwean got 200 asylum seekers into UK for £2000.00 each. Yes, I now believe Black, Asia, and other Ethnic Minority in Britain are causing criminal activities in British society and have created pressure to British police.'

'Three Asian Britons made at least £2 millions. As part of UK massive counterfeit operation were jailed for producing and selling fake Viagra tablets in UK chemists, some fake Viagra were sold legitimately over the counter in Britain on prescription and some sent to US and other countries. Viagra is used for treating men sex problems. Therefore, you can buy fake drugs in approved chemists in civilised Britain of 21st century.'

'A British super-rich billionaire couple's heir to £5.4 billion organisation was charged in connection to heroin and crack cocaine smuggled into a reception at US embassy at London. What a confused family, what a confused society.'

'A British granddad, 72 years old convicted of raping and abusing nine girls age 6 to 13 years. The granddad started having sex with one of the teenage at age seven with promises of ice cream, the teenage told the court.'

'Two level examination papers were in circulation 2 weeks before the due date. Some students are buying the stolen questions and then selling them on. An uncivilised issue of developing country in developed Britain.'

'A British man 27-years-old claiming and calling himself son of god in internet has 76,000 images and 1,000 videos on his computer of sex activities of babies being tortured and raped. The children and babies sex club has 700 men members. Men have sex with babies 2 to 5-years-old in their rooms while other members watch them via internet in their home computer. British civilised society should remember that the internet has no boundary. Is pornography a civilised way of behaviour? In Africa, 95 percent of the people do not know what pornography is, are Britons just teaching Africa wrong or right things?'

'A British furniture dealer killed and chopped up his best friend's arm after a drinking binge, roasted the arm in an oven and then fled to USA, a court heard.'

'A young British Asian boy was killed by 50 white men for being an Asian. In another case three British Asian men who burned a school boy alive just because he was white were jailed by the court.'

'A British Barrister who teamed up with gangsters to turn his apartment into a cocaine factory has been jailed for seven years and cocaine worth £150,000 found. I thought a barrister must be among civilised human's group, a barrister selling and dealing in drug in 21st century.'

'Two British heroin addicts fed their toddler son methadone (drug) for five years before he died of an overdose. Another British heroin addict, a father of two, claiming nearly £80,000 in benefits for 36 children has being jailed for 13 months. In Britain, a singer openly smokes a joint (cannabis) on TV interview. The same singer was arrested some days ago after being found slumped at the wheel of his car for the second time this year because of cannabis in-take but was not jailed. If he was a common person, he would be sent to prison. Britain is glamorising drug-user celebrities in 21st century causing more children to take drugs and have mentally related issues like shooting and stabbing. Sixty cannabis farms are raided every month in London area, police reviewed. Now, cannabis leaves are produced more in Britain's society than in the Caribbean. Two British women and a man held after tragic waste of life, a ten-years-old girl has died after taking ecstasy they kept in their house. The young are even victim of the drug in Britain. Another British mother gave her nine year old son wraps of heroin to take to school and made sure he got his hit, get high at school. Some rotten British parent should take care of their rotten children and rotten parent should be blamed for their children's rotten behaviour. Again, a British aristocrat faces 15 years jail term in USA over chain gang drugs allegation dating back more than 20 years ago. He was accused of being involved in a plot to smuggle £60 million of cannabis from Caribbean to the USA.'

'A 64-years-old British hotel boss hid a camera in a hotel bedroom so he could watch costumers having sex in 21st century British civilised society.'

'Two French students in London were tied-up, tortured, stabbed 245 times in the head, neck, back, chest, torso in a horrific murder before their flat was firebombed. Why are people behaving badly in a civilised society?'

'A model pupil was stabbed to death in a London park by another boy because he was wearing the uniform of a rival school, what a senseless attack. Another British girl was kicked to death in a public park by a mob when she tried to stop them from attacking her boyfriend.'

'Two London teenage girls were jailed in Ghana for trying to smuggle cocaine into the UK, Britons in drug distribution in uncivilised society in 21st century, what a shame. Another British teenager who took a fatal dose of ecstasy was extremely high and had white foam in his mouth for more than three hours was dragged from a house and left to die in the streets by partygoers. Where is the civilised British society?'

'A young British father 23-years-old was stabbed repeatedly to death on a dance floor in front of hundreds of horrified clubbers and in another incident, a new dad died after he was stabbed in a row over a girl at a party.'

'A 57-years-old sick British father was punched to the face and he collapsed in supermarket floor and died, why are people from civilised society becoming so angry?'

'A British man 52-years-old gassed his daughter 7-years-old and son 3-years-old to death after break-up with wife.'

'About 7 British urban areas in flood and more than 70,000 Britons made homeless for weeks and months. How can people from civilised society plan and build houses on flood plains. Are British people not civilised in house planning? Why granting building permission on flood plains, more rainfall seasons are coming, corrupt officers – corruption in civilised society. British society need houses and lands made available for building houses and then what is wrong? Local plain lands for housing in exchange for bribes. 'Why Africans deal in civilised British society?'

'A woman was sexually assaulted alongside a busy road, as passing drivers ignored her screams – why?'

'A juror was caught smuggling drugs and a crack pipe into a high security London court where a 7th July London bombing trial was under way, an uncivilised act you cannot see in an uncivilised society.'

'British grave robbers, 73 plaques was stolen from crematorium in Enfield area and later dumped in an industrial estate because it will only fetch between £100 and £300 if melted down, what a confused robbers. In addition, thieves ripping lead off church roofs to sell for scrap in 21st century British society, it is ridiculous, has the civilised society gone mad?'

'A teenager was chased through a packed city centre by a knife-wielding mob that stabbed him to death as they caught him, just like killing a robber in African society. Another shocking video, showing where a woman with mentally related disability collapses and died in waiting room floor while hospital staffs ignored her, what a confused British society. Where are civilised European and British society, do we have civilised individuals and not civilised society?'

I must not be force pretending that Britain is not a confused society with many uncivilised events everywhere like other Africans who have been in Britain and force pretend about Britain's bad behaviour.' I am against crime, fighting crime that costs each taxpayer £275 including myself in each given year and £15 billion in total in each given year. Government blaming parents for recent increase in children's bad behaviour, yet I do not know how to instil discipline in my children because the same government removed corporal punishment from parents and schools and imposed restrictions on the police, so we do not know how to discipline this unfruitful children. I have seen civilisation and bad events fell back in love and married in British society, a civilised society with discrimination and bad behaviour. What is then a civilised society? A civilised society with 1,046,437 recorded violent crimes in 2007 in England area alone, just like uncivilised society of Nigeria. What is making people from civilised society behaviour in this bad way – knifing every given 4 minutes and 130,000 blade attacks in the year 2007? About more than 30 youngsters were murdered by their follow youngsters in year 2007 with gun or knife in Britain's civilised society. I'm still not near to knowing what have caused the Britons bad behaviour and I cannot believe with some of the things I am seeing if I am in Britain – with such uncivilised events. Please watch your step, front and back once you are with some Britons, things may not be as angelic as you hoped. 'Two teenagers kicked defenceless stranger man in southeast London to death for no reason 'just a man who was looking at them in a civilised society.' Inside myself I said 'this tale of uncivilised issues in a civilised society is not a comfortable story however, it is an important one that demands to be read as we all like to live in a civilised society. Yes, we cannot change the past misbehaviours however, knowing the past behaviour we sometimes feels ashamed and manage our future well.' Why when it comes to behaviour, people from civilised society will need more rehabilitation support than people from uncivilised society do? Then what is civilised society? Parents advice children and give them the good lifestyle they deserve – protect your loved one's future with advice. 'Parents advice and support at family home, the gift of children lifetime and the knowledge that shapes our society.' However, with the above catalogue of human errors that shamed civilised societies, do we have civilised or confused society in Europe and America nations?

Confused Society

My granddad and dad told me that Europe and United States of America are civilised societies. Is Europe and US deliberately understating the size of it barbaric or unrefined behaviour in the 21st century, seen by some as the root cause of some of the world barbarous problems? However, 'I have come to Britain nation to see white coloured British people but I am seeing light pink colour British, where have the white coloured British people I was told about their white colour in African gone? I want to see black coloured British people but what I am seeing is light brown people not black in colour – no pure coloured white or black, what a confused world.' Is Europe a civilised society, what a joke? Can we have civilised society with some of the people with confused behaviour then what is civilised society? I think we have civilised individuals and not civilised society in Britain. Many white and black British people are lacking basic life skills such as having daily bath or shower – unable to dress well, talk and behave well in public places but there are perfectly healthy people who work or enter public places yet with poverty life skills trained in a civilised society. How can a co-worker be smells like alcohol or cigarette worker in the office every time in none alcohol or cigarette base project? Some workers coming to work place under the influence of substance-alcohol and drugs in a civilised society. 'Civilised society which means moving out of savagery or barbarism into a moral refinement in culture and education, or enlighten behaviour.' However, Britain has been the source of more bad news than good news since I reached London. The main gossip in the society is all about drug dealers, yobs culture, organised crimes, alcohol and drugs misusing celebrities and ethnic minority group issues they see and hear in media and newspapers. The government departments planning and doing well to the society betterment but some of the citizens refuse the government support and behave badly like animals. Britain is a civilised society because of high science and technology items they make and use, but a confused society because of the uncivilised events in a civilised society. 'Britain society brings home to me how civilised I am.' Britain is a confused society for having civilised and uncivilised events at the same time. However, can we have a civilised society with bad behaviours? Britain, what a confused society, a nation of terrorist suspects, adult and child alcohol abuse, stabbing and shooting, discrimination, money laundering and credit problems – need a drink get a new credit card or need to eat-out get a new credit card. The British society, who likes to glorify people for their immoral behaviour and activities, singers with drug problems and run-ins with the police are in the media and newspapers in each given week. British media glamorising alcohol and drug user celebrities with confused teenagers thinking it is the right way to be popular. 'I had my first cigarette when I was seven at the outbreak of the First World War in 1914. I am giving up my cigarettes smoking lifestyle after 95 years said a 102 Briton mum, and the main headline news in all the British newspapers that week – so some confused teenagers thinking cigarettes smoking keep you live longer.' 'Britain has more binge drinkers than any leading nation – Britons are worst in world for teen bingeing.' The British Medical Association, has called for a blanket ban on any alcohol brand name sport events by alcohol companies – claiming Britain to be a nation of drunks tottering around and smashing each other face with broken bottles, causing more problems to individual, family and the health sectors, so if we stop alcohol companies from sponsoring their own company sport events, we will be sober up at once and become 'a great nation again.' Then why most of the British media comments that booze ban in Britain is a bad news.

The media claiming that doctors are not what they use to be, before if you have infection they will carry out medical test before treatment but now they give tablets on presumption for you to take care of yourself at home. Once upon a time doctors knew everything – now they do not know the effect of alcohol companies sponsoring sport on our society said the media. If alcohol companies pull their undoubted millions out of sport, it will leave a massive hole that will be impossible to fill – that with or without alcohol companies sponsoring sport events we still have to face and die of heart disease. However, 'without alcohol company's sponsors, sport will lose out, in turn we will all start to get fat and die – so no alcohol company's money no sport, we get fat and die.' So why do we British complain of a generation of teen alcohol culture since alcohol money is good for our sport and health. Who do us trust, the British Medical Association or the British Medias? What a confused issue, we are in confused society. In addition, London Booze ban strike on public transport puts underground train beyond the law and I spent two hours in an underground train, just half way to next station. I descended from the underground in Edgware road station, thirsty and in need of toilet room, the underground stations has no toilet room or water for passengers as one station officer told me, in a civilised society. 'No toilet room for travellers in a train station in civilised society.' More than 8000 adults in London that night strike chants 'leave our booze alone', yet more than 3000 youngsters are being treated in hospitals in each given year. Booze-alcohol is the greatest problem in British schools than drugs, knife, gun or school financing. 'Therefore, children say 'adults go bingeing all the time and they are normal', so children follow them. Children are now behaving like adults and carry knife to protect themselves since they faces adult's funs which is leading to horrific rise in knife crime.' The pictures of people doing the public alcohol strike appear clearly in almost all the newspapers, what action did the London Mayor and Police take. 'A British man just speaking English in England can never be granted as an achievement in Britain.' As children behave like adult, common house tool like domestic or kitchen knives becomes the biggest killers in British society. 'Just a dirty look at a British teenage gang you may be stabbed to death by the teenagers.' What a confused British society. Britain, a generation of fear society where children cannot move freely within their community because of child sex abuse and killing of children for fun in a British civilised society, is this a civilised behaviour, harming children, our future hope. 'Three Britons have been arrested after the remains of three newborn babies, thought to have been hidden since the 1980s, were found in September 2009.' Civilised societies were children suppose to have freedom of movement but children are now hidden in rooms, we are in confused society. 'What kind of country has Britain becomes when we are all treated as potential paedophiles – if you are hosting family children or school parties, helping out with lifts of children, driving other people children to events, you will become a criminal unless you consent to the Independent Safeguarding Authority vetting you.' When did all Britons become paedophiles? When Britain did becomes a nation of paedophiles? However, 'the feeling when you lost a child or relative is deep but should our children be protecting themselves with weapons.' One in 10 British pupils has seen or is being attacked with a weapon-knife or air pistol. Sixteen weapons – six knives, a metal baseball bat, a mental golf club, a corkscrew, a mallet, a metal bar and two screwdrivers was seized on one bus from a teenage gang aged between 14 and 18. The 24 youths were preparing for a fight with another gang elsewhere in London. What will the violence children are in coming 20 years, people from civilised, uncivilised, or confuse society? London police have carried out almost 27,000 stops-and- searches in just six weeks between May/ June 2008, almost 1000 of the suspects stopped were arrested for carrying knives or other weapons and more than 250 were arrest for involvement in knife crime. Why can't civilised people behave in civilised ways in civilised society? The police search in their bid to curb the capital's knife-crime epidemic. Eight teenagers dead within 48 hours in Britain in knife hate crime. Top British politicians ban selling knife to kids but three teenagers went and bought 33 knifes in a day. What a confused society. Politicians blaming greedy and rude parents for their children's behaviour in the street and not blaming shopkeepers for selling knifes to teenagers and government not putting curfew on children's movement at night through their parents. Even, a female member of parliament 50 years-old becomes Britain's victim of live-threatening beating by a vicious gang of thugs. She suffered head injuries, several broken ribs and had several bruising on leg and hand. As she lay unconscious, the teenage yobs take her gold watch and chain, diamond ring and stud earring from her. Is this type of confused group of yobs or thugs naming it what you like, among civilised British society. 'So are the parents of the teenagers rotten or the teenagers rotten – rotten parents should take care of their rotten children. Parents should report their rotten children or they would be considered, as being rotten parents.' Some internet pictures of stabbed victims with guns and knives and yet they claimed to been innocent once they are killed by fellow gang members. We are in a confused society, how do we know when a rotten child or gang child is killed with this British knife culture. Families live in fear as kids are killing kids, can this be the type of society Asians and

Africans have been hoping to reach – teenage savagery culture, we are in confused society.

How can I tell the story that a civilised and rich Britain has issues related to homelessness – roofless issues? Why having street rough sleepers in a civilised and rich British society? 'UK government claiming to have only 500 streets rough sleepers yet cannot house them. Why a civilised and rich society can't house its citizen with mental disability issues?' A civilised society council with street rough sleepers and homelessness unit, what is civilised society then? Why can't people in a civilised society know how to behave or manager their housing issues well? Homelessness issues at British decent homes. Where is the decent home I was told about British society? I went to the British countryside and could not believe the number of people who are poor and facing with issues related to homelessness in civilised society. 'Ten foreign workers living in 2-bed rooms flat with one toilet room and one kitchen room. 'Foreign workers lived below African and Asian standard of living in a civilised British society.' 'Emergency urinating is always a problem, you keep waiting for a door slam to notice that the toilet room is free to be used or you urinate in a small bottle and cover it until the toilet room is free for you to throw it away, just like you are imprisoned in a rented accommodation in Britain's 21st century.' Britons Building new houses with wooden floor and wooden wall, people moving and talking in one flat or house disturbing its neighbours - noise and no privacy, issues related to homelessness even in newly built houses. Rooms like tiny shoeboxes. Why are issues related to homelessness developing in homeless projects in civilised society? 'Homelessness issues at government approved home-hostels, what is home then?' A mentally-ill homeless people live in mentally-ill homeless project but when they behave like people with mental disability like having challenging behaviour, broken house rules and verbally abusive or use of insulting languages to staff, they evict them to streets, so making more homeless people, homeless people they suppose to support and fight their homelessness related issues. 'I never wash my inside room wall, then why should I tell homeless people to be washing their room wall three times in each given year than painting the wall with the organisation money.' When will a street mentally homeless person behave like a person with mentally related issues in a mental hostel, the hostel will not call police station, may be from police cell to the hospital and then to the streets as a mentally homeless person once again. Why do we have mental health hostels if we will not employ professionally qualified mental health professional in the hostel to manage client's problems directly. A mental health related accommodation project site without a qualified mental worker – no mental trained nurse, social worker, or housing disability practitioner in 21st century British society. Yet those who study mental health in University have no job and yet unqualified workers are paid higher wages than qualified workers, there still remain many questions to answer why employ and pay unqualified white Britons higher than qualified ethnic people – job connection, corruption and discrimination in 21st century British society. What a confused society. Homeless accommodation projects that cannot offer rough sleepers room in their hostel. Homeless supported housing projects with no professionally qualified care or housing workers or practitioners in their hostels. Where are the trained workers – driving buses, cleaners, or claiming state benefit? Thus, British organisations force pretending to be helping people with mental disability just to get contract, grant, and money from the government and organisations for their personal gain in 21st century civilised British society. Britain supported housing in a culture of carelessness, a client with mental disability refused going for his medication prescription and staff refused going for his medication. For four weeks, the client did not take his medication. Staff reason for not going for the client medication prescription is that if the client can come for his breakfast, lunch and dinner then he can as well go out for his medication prescription from the local health team. Therefore, staff discouraging mentally ill clients from eating food, which staff supposed to encouraged them to take.

'I have learnt to trust people in civilised society whatever they do for a living.' Homeless people in care in supported housing without having to bath or shower for months, People in supported homes and civilised society who suppose to bath or shower daily are now source of infection disease like Methicillin-resistant staphylococcus aureus, Clostridium Difficile, Tuberculosis, and Hepatitis C. It is a surprise to see and smell homeless people as they near you in public places in civilised British society of the 21st century. If housing, supporting and care workers do not take care of their residents and tenants, who will take care of them? Housing, supporting and care projects staff should bury their heads in shame. 'Street homeless people falling homeless while homeless at homeless people hostel.' 'Homeless people developing homelessness related issues in homeless people hostel why? Hostel that suppose to fight homeless people issues now, are causing more homelessness issues to homeless people.' Streets rough sleepers, British people who do not have room to sleep at night but inside cartoons in the street corridors, I thought Britain was a rich society. Physical conditions and unhygienic state of their resting places of the streets rough sleepers pose great health and environmental hazards for Britain and world societies as you can see homeless people in train stations and airports, people travelling can carry their leftover to other countries. 'Homeless people are a bit of an eyesore and are having a negative effect in Britain as a civilised society.' Some of the homeless hostels for people with disability have no professionally trained worker with professional qualifications to deal with their residents issues directly, shock and disbelief in 21st century British society. 'Streets rough sleepers with complex and multiple needs without professionally qualified workers working with them in hostels.' Still many unanswered questions on why organisations do not offer job to professionally qualified and experienced workers but to unqualified workers. How do I tell home people in Africa that a wealthy and civilised country like Britain is still having people with issues related to homelessness – roofless issues – people sleeping on the streets in a civilised society? Are this street homeless people among the civilised British society? What is civilised society? 'In a civilised society' for one to be house by council homelessness unit you must be force-pretending as you are suffering from mentally related issues such as sleeping rough/drinking on the streets as to be in council homelessness unit priority list' absolutely horrified news. However, all homeless people charity organisation claiming to be opening doors for homeless people but street rough sleepers have to pass through council homelessness unit waiting list and complete benefit housing benefit claim form before the council or charity organisations can house them. 'Street rough sleepers, people with mental disability, who like to be master of the streets being ask to fill housing application form or an assessment form before they leave the streets, council homelessness unit and charity organisations must be joking.' We are in confused society. MPs, many have second homes from my money and other taxpayers that remain empty for much or all the year and some people sleeping rough on the street in a civilised society, why? MPs, unless more is done to break the link between mental health and homelessness, British society will still have street rough sleeper. 'The MPs bogus expenses scandal was honourable unbelievable breach of trust between the MP and British/world society.' MPs do honourable thing and pay the claims back as stipulated by the government auditor and street rough sleepers may have a first home with your repayment than sleeping on the streets. Restaurant workers scorn and turn street rough sleepers away around their sites for begging – they are sober and asking for food not drink, yet people left their half eaten meal on plates that could have filled so many empty stomachs but are throw away. Why the local council cannot give the street people the right help, in the right place at the right time and the thrown away food will be for street homeless people, so manage street lifestyles well in a rich and civilised society? However, one group of people begging for food to live and causing anti-social behaviour in a civilised society and another group people throwing food away because of they are commercial sectors and paying tax, which group do we support? Which of the group are causing problem to our society? What a confused question and society. However, who should manage street rough sleepers' issues as charity organisations are having allegations of budget-breaking, improper relationship between staff and staffs, staffs and customers, and making profit. When is a charity organisation not a charity organisation needs to pay tax, stop begging or its profit use for customer welfare?

Why can't a civilised society clean and manage its recycle rubbish well? What a dirty and stinking London summer period, compost centre stench in North London near my house, and visiting fish and meat market with foul odour and flies all over which left buyers vomiting, causes by warm weather like that of the African dry season. I thought civilised society should know what to do with change in climate. London lorry waste remover so smelly that, some time left me vomiting as the lorry neared my house collecting rubbish. Can't they wash the Lorries, can't Britons smell the dirty odour from the Lorries, so Britons do not notice the bad odour from the lorry. The story of a body boy is found dead in a bin liner is painful, what a British society shameful act. The body of a newborn baby boy was found in a bin liner on a conveyor belt at waste recycling plant – Britons dumping human body in the back of recycling lorry, what a confused society.

My area local council provide 3 boxes for separate rubbish recycle items – cans, glass, plastic, and paper. I sort rubbish into boxes, then its all dump in together into the back of a dustcart – rubbish lorry in front of my house as we watch. Then why do we bother about recycle? What a confused society? In Germany, you return an empty bottle and you get money from the shop, which has made some German people to pick or take their litter for money but in Britain, nobody cares because our litter does not make money. Even some British council want you to pay for collecting rubbish from your door step. A white British lady 83-years-old in Enfield reporting to news agency about 50 bags of reeking rubbish left to rot outside a block of flats for three weeks and were uncollected by Enfield council. The rubbish bags leave residents facing stinking household waste of dirty nappies and cans of food that you walk pass without gag. The bin bags broke open and birds and cats were getting to feed on them – that is why Britain is a nation of animal lovers. Even, 'In front of my house overfilled rubbish bins from supermarkets can be left for two months – keeping cat, fox, and rats happy.' I have been to other European countries such as Switzerland and Germany surprised at how clean their towns and countryside are, but Britain is full of rubbish, dumping rubbish in streets and ignoring recycling. I am now facing issues related to homelessness in my house. In front of my house are post office and

Muslim school/mosque, and at backside of my house is a car park which attracts space for rubbish dumping and rats are now visiting my compound. Two minutes walk from my house is a nightclub, fast food shops, and late night closing pub – beer bar and people urinating in front of my house at night, I am now living in civilised hell society. 'A dirty street pavements caused by fast food, chewing gum, and cigarette ends litter, dogs fouling.' 'Why is the city pavements dotted with chewing gum and half eating cartoons of food in a civilised society? Is this a civilised behaviour – dirty pavements?' In Britain, about 200,000 demonstrators are protesting about climate change in London area, each of demonstrators has a flag made of cloth or paper posters. After the protest, the streets were full of about 100 to 500 tons of rubbish adding more problems to the climate. What a confused society. A government that is fighting for climate change but keeps its offices' light on for 24 hours even when people are not working in the offices, half empty buses, trains, and planes has been seen moving to different long distances causing more harm to the climate. A British security van has made 120-mile trip to take a prisoner 200 yards because walking a prisoner across a road with handcuffs breaches the human rights law. What a confused society, wasting my money and other taxpayers' money. I thought Britain supports world agenda on climate change and need to encourage people to walk. I have a car but I cannot park in front of my house, not because of space in front of my house to park my car but I have to pay before I park in front of my house by using parking permit machine which I pay £2 per hour and not parking for more than two hours in each given period as the council do not issue resident park permit to people living in high road. So I have to be changing the position of my car in each given two hours then causing more harm to the climate. I am paying my road tax, MOT tax, community rent tax on my flat and need a car for my work as my employer need their staff to drive in case of emergency visit to clients. Britain is fighting against climate change and I could use the public transport better than my car for work but my employer wants me to come to work with my car. Why must I have to pay for parking my car in front of my house and come to work with a car than using better public transport, still many unanswered questions? Yet the same organisations or government departments has nearly 25 to 100 page sheets on recycle and climate change. What a confused society. British government department saying use water, do not waste it – using the hose unnecessarily wastes 16 litres of water a minute – using a bucket and sponge instead of a hose uses less water, protects the environment and could save you money. Yet British local councils are approving all car washers to use hose than bucket and sponge – what a confused society.

In 21st century, everywhere you go in Europe we hear slavery is an outdated issue. Yet, one in ten Britons use prostitutes and Britain has about 25,000 sex slaves. Slavery still exists today as thousands of Eastern Europeans, Africans and Asians still force themselves into the British society. Before Britons go to Africa and force them to Europe but now Eastern Europeans, Africans and Asians force themselves to British cities. The slave trade was mostly for cheap labour for Americans and Europeans. British government ended involvement in the trans-Atlantic slave trade, British Prime Minister apologises for Britain's part in slave trade and said in my own words, 'my sorrow at the slave (black) trade, Africa slave trade is one of the most in-human enterprises in history.' Africa families sold family members as a source to get money for a living and today family encourage other member to visit another country for any unaccepted work or job because of money. Slavery has re-emerged in different ways in Britain, as about 85 per cent of females working in brothels – prostitution house for British men, has been trafficked, working and living in slum conditions in Britain, young women of 14 – 18-years-old have sex to about 10 to 20 British men in each given night. The consequence is that white British women have followed in the sex trade, for just £5 to £10, you have a drop with a white women in my area between midnight to 4 am as they pretend to be waiting/coming out of nightclubs.

Is British Prime Minister apologising just in words and not in practical, in 21st century British society in another form of slavery trade - what a shame. A British just speaking English, I do not think that should be achievement, 'Speaking English language can never be an achievement in England an Englishman land.' A British teenage girl 16-years-old waiting for a bus was forced into Kensington gardens and raped; the attack took place about 01:25 night hours. The police investigating officer saying the attack was serious that has left the girl traumatised but did not warn teenage girls not to go out or stay out at night. My question is what a girl of 16-years-old was doing outside their family house at 01:25 am, seeing which friends for alcohol, drug or prostitution. Why civilised society parents can't put curfew to their teenagers at dark hours. Where are the British decent family lifestyles I have come to see in UK? In east London, a boy of 14-years-old weds girl of 13 years-old both from Polish Gypsy wedding in Britain. The lads even observed the gypsy custom of having sex with the bride the night before the ceremony. Where are the Britain police and child protection agency? British home office said the ceremony has no standing in law – but pictures of the wedding are in national newspapers. The 13 years-old girl said that she now feels like a proper grown-up since she is living together with her husband a 14 years-old boy. The mother of the 13-years-old girl is above the British law claiming that she married at the age of 14-years-old through such a ceremony, it has not done her any harm and does not care about what neighbours and social services think. The girl's mother said, that living in Britain does not mean she has to behave in the way British people think is right, that her life is her life and she would bring her kids up in her own way of life. Is this bride at 13-years-old cause by poverty as we noticed, that the parent could not afford to pay their house rent, send his five kids to school and her parent living in two-bed rooms flat with other fourteen relatives? Between British culture and Polish Gypsy culture, which one is better? Britain, why not solves your own society's problem before looking into other countries society problems – child sex abuse in 21st century in Britain society. 'BBC showing Nigeria teen marriage disadvantages to British people in the Television, yet Britain have teen marriage problem.' Is Gypsy community not among the civilised European society? Is Polish community not among the civilised Europeans? British and European societies having child bride and child sex abuse in the 21st century society, what a shame? An act you see in African and Asian villages, now in London city. What will Europeans tell Africans and Asians about child mismanagement? 'A newborn baby two-days-old girl with her umbilical cord still attached dumped in bushes near a supermarket in Britain.' What is a civilised society with more

British young girls becoming more pregnant and single mother than girls in developing country - uncivilised society do? Are these young British women with three children from three different fathers among the British civilised society? Most of the children have no father, no family training, becomes future British stabbing and shooting generation, having children as to get high state benefit and support services like early Africans of 17th and 18th century having many children to help them in farming, a society in crisis. 'Young women in civilised society having children from different men is becoming a civilised culture in civilised society, whatever you do in civilised society is always civilised life styles' About 3000 kids of 'sex pest schoolchildren' are suspended or excluded for horrific incidents that included sexual assaults, sexual abuse, sexual harassment, sexual bulling, sex attacks on teachers and every ten minutes a knife crime is committed and it is rising in Britain's civilised society. What a confused society. 'A white British girl admitted that she lost her virginity at 16-years-old and at 18-years-old has slept with more than 50 men, that she cannot remember some of their names – white colour prostitution.' Britain's nationwide crime committed by girl's ages between 10 and 17 has rose to 12 per cent in 2007 and in Enfield where I live, crime committed by girls has soared to nearing 40 per cent. British girls drinking alcohol more but unable handle it at such a young age has contributed a very large part to their crime activity. Young British boys befriending fellow British young girls and passing them to older men, trading in girls 'sex' – prostitution in 21st century. 'Is boob or breasts plastic surgery a civilised act, British women showing their chest by wearing low-cut dress, V-dress and nipple grazing top as to show their plastic surgery increased breast. What good have I learnt in this confused British society of 21st century?' Uncivilised issues developing in America, Europe, Asia, and Africa societies in the 21st century - a societies separated by distance, it is the same selflessness behaviour that makes America and Europe confused societies like uncivilised society of Asia and Africa. Uncivilised issues happening in civilised society do amazes me till today however, you learn a lot about yourself when you failed – my coming to live in Europe society. Moreover, the quickest way to know the quality of a society is by being there. 'A civilised society like University is the future because it prepares you to learn and do new things.' However, world's most sinful cities is also in civilised societies, cities like Majorca, London, Los Angeles, Sydney, Las Vegas, Amsterdam notorious for their sex shop, strip clubs, drug overdoes issues, 24 hours gambling centres, red light district, streets alcohol and drug rough sleepers. Yes, there are civilised society, romantic, and sexy cities and then there are packed with all that is bed for human living. 'There is something wrong with civilisation, the uncivilised issues developing in civilised societies, what a confused world?' The most prolific criminal in UK, a crack addict prostitute with 700 convictions, 36 years old white Briton live in Brixton's notorious red light district in south London. She has used the district since she was a teenager, Police knows her and knows her business and has her pictures working and yet nothing is been done. The prostitute has sex for £10 and they spent the money on drugs within a few minutes. In addition, news and fears as fifth British prostitute vanishes and later five British women are dead in Suffolk area. They are street sex women age 19 – 29 years old, selling sex for money to the public in the streets in 21st century civilised British society. I am now confused about what a rich and civilised society is. Do we have a rich society or an individually rich people? What a confused society.

The British society is in a serious problem with issues related to obesity and overweight, about 15 per cents of 15-years-old and one in ten schoolchildren are overweight. It is called national epidemic and Britain's national health services approved free treatment and drugs. Yet you visit British hostels, hospitals, schools, restaurants and family homes you see people cooking and eating English breakfast or Saturday fry that is made of 8 to 12 saturated fat items. Why can't people from civilised society know what is good and not good for their body. What a confused society. People keep buying food without eating it could be funny – civilised society who throw away one third of the food they bought while some families have no food to eat, an act you cannot see in uncivilised society of Africa and Asia family, Africa and Asia's joint family system are better. You will see Notices in all the British public places saying – every 5 minutes someone has a stroke in Britain, reduce your chances of having a stroke – don't smoke, eat healthy, and drink sensibly yet, you see people smoking cigarettes, eating fast food, and drinking alcohol openly in the streets.' What a confused society. In Britain, a civilised society of 21st century, the government and health practitioners are saying smoking kills and causes lung cancer, chronic obstructive pulmonary disease, heart disease and other cancer – of the month, nose, larynx, and kidney. However, you see people smoking outside their office buildings, public places and even in the hospital premises, SMOKERS - PLEASE MIND THE FRESH FREE AIR FROM GOD. Why do people from civilised society not know what is good or not good for their body. Who says we have a civilised society with all the people not behaving well must be lie that won't die. 'Society show me a well behave society manners without disgusting issues, I will call you a civilised society.' Why in Britain, Obesity-overweight declared as public enemy number one in a civilised society, 'why can't people know what is good or bad for their body.' Britain is a nation of food who loves books, DVD, and Television programmes about food eating but most of us still can't cook for ourselves however, have obsession with cheap food like fizzy drinks and crisps, and fast food like chips and burgers. We are in a confused world.

Why discrimination officially in British politics, 'a constitution of one of the British political party does not believe non-white people, even if they were born in Britain, can ever really be British. The party stands for the preservation of the national and ethnic character of the British and is wholly opposed to any form of racial integration between British and non-European people. They affirm that non-whites has no place in Britain at all and will not rest until every last one has left Britain soil – they banned mixed-race relationship.' The political party allowed only white Britons to be their members – yet Britain have policy on discrimination and nothing is been done to fight the politics party policy and procedure by the government than not involving them in some meetings. The British Broadcasting Corporation 'BBC' was under fire from anti-racist groups for its invitation to the British National Party 'BNP' – you must be white in colour to be their party member. BBC was also heavily criticised after a Radio 1 programme allowed two BNP officials to declare that black England-born England footballers were not really English. What a confused society.

Patients, who were denied drugs are dying in the hospital because of cost of drugs, I thought Britain is a rich society. Where was the British National Health Service and local primary care trusts and where are the trusts and services? Britain's national health services hospitals are full of primary care related issues – hospital uncleanness leading to infection diseases spreading. The Local primary care trusts are full of national related issues, refusing new drugs by NHS finance leading to patients waiting for new drugs treatment approval until they died and the drugs will be available after patient's death. However, once a Trust is slam by a local group of people after death of a patient then that is the only way of getting a new drug approval in a civilised society. What a confused society.

In UK, nearly 3,900 women in labour had to give birth outside a maternity unit in each given year, often because there were no space beds – some tots were delivered in family homes, hospital corridors, lifts and even toilets. What a confused society.

Civilised society British Muslims saying that 'if you mess-up with Islamic religion in Britain, you will be a target and killed to highlight injustice against Muslims across the world.' Please confused killers, answer your father's name, no killing in the name of British Muslims society. No killing in the name of Allah or God. However, at the same time a Muslim community leader was kidnapped from his home at knifepoint and ordered to stop holding prayer sessions after a 'white only allow members' political party hate campaign. 'I have no problem with Islamic ideology and Islamic culture, but I have come to England to see English culture.' So UK is no longer safe haven for decent Muslim people but a confused society for them. 'Is a multi-cultural society, a multi-confusing society?' What is multicultural British society? Another Muslim man was attacked outside a mosque, just days after a pensioner died following a race-hate assault. The attack came just 24 hours after a 67-years-old man died following a similar assault less than a mile away. I thought Britons claimed to be living in a multicultural society? London female Muslims says Yes to Hijabs. London Doctors says No to Hijabs claiming those Muslim women who wear the Hijabs are at risk of serious illness because they do not get enough sun as a result suffer from vitamin D deficiency. Human body vitamin D, which prevents rickets, is obtain through exposure to sunlight and only a little comes from food, can civilisation work well with culture, religion or science? Many London female Muslims still wear Hijabs claiming the London doctors are racist. London doctors saying, 'we are not racist and we have nothing against Muslims but concern about their health.' Is human civilisation a conflict of groups' interest between different cultures? We are in a confused society. White British killing Muslim

British and Muslim British killing white British. What a confused world.

What is wrong in a British society with a very good transportation system in London? Why can't we have peace on London public transport system, too loud music from personal music device systems in bus and train? Many children shouting, screaming, pushing, playing loud music, swearing, and dancing on buses and trains - thinking that they can get away with misbehaving because of their age and the law. Britons standing and drinking cups of coffee or tea on moving bus and train – PLEASE MIND MY CLOTHES. In civilised society, people shout when they talk on a mobile phone in public areas, putting their dirty bags and feet on bus and train seats, eating smelly food and dropping litter in a public buses and trains. It is very intimidating seeing people openly drinking alcohol in bus and train, I always think they have mentally related issues but they claim it is British culture, if it is British culture then all Britons must need alcohol treatment. 'Yes, it is British cultural lifestyle for I have seen London city mayors walking, eating, and drinking on the streets, on moving buses and trains.' One-hour working break, you see workers going to drink alcohol in pub, after work, you see the same workers going for a drink in pub. Going home, you see the same workers with cans of beer, workers smelling alcoholic in offices. Why leave empty alcohol cans and bottles inside public buses and trains? I asked one white Briton to pick the litters he left in the train floor and he asked me, what would the cleaners be doing? I think some parents or adult are to blame, none of the adults sitting in the train helped me as the man tried to attack me, they all sat and kept reading their free newspapers – BRITAIN, A NATION OF FREE MORNING AND EVENING NEWSPAPERS. It is acceptable for people having problem to drink bottle water or soft drinks while on public transport but consumption of hot or cold food such as pasties, burger, kebabs, sandwiches, chips, or drinking beer and other alcohol is not acceptable – it smells a lot. I thought Britons from Black, Asia, and Ethnic minority only do this mess but white Britons do it more. Is this a civilised culture? What an uncivilised attack on modern London transport system – an average of eight crimes like stabbings, sexual assaults, beatings and as well as 160 cases of criminal damages, flights, fare disputes and drunken clashes by gangs are reported each day in London buses. Some unreported incidents include schoolchildren opening and closing door of moving buses on traffic jam, sometime you can be afraid that they might be among the London teenagers gang but are in school uniform. Is this type of group of gang and confused individuals among civilised British society? What is civilised society? In Britain, you will see notice on all moving train doors 'EMERGENCY USE DOOR ONLY' danger – risk of death if used when train is moving or obstructing the doors can be dangerous when train is moving and yet you see Britons using and obstructing the doors as the trains are moving. Even white Britons obstructing door of moving trains – is this a civilised behaviour? What a confused society.

A 62, 000 tonne ship-napoleon deliberately beaches on British coast and 200 containers fell into the sea. Police have attempted to block access to the beaches but plenty of scavengers have come tooled up to the beach and ready to take advantage. Police warns off ship scavengers and coastguard condemns greed of the looters but more British scavengers come to the beach. More than 1000 British scavengers on the beach celebrate funding some washed-up car steering, packs of nappies, BMW bike, dog food, mobile phones. Some of the goods plundered from the napoleon's container are already on sale on eBay and described on the auction website as recovered from Bran comber village and one seller even mentioned of not knowing if the items work or not, but it's expensive to buy new one. One UK police chief says – it is safe to leave your door open in Britain. Police officer, you are just joking – I can't leave my door open for this type of Britain's civilised society. The fact that London police officers still refuse to patrol any street single-handed, as once they did in 1960 as claimed by my 70-years-old white Briton service user shows how unsafe British communities are now. I am just in confused mood but the police claiming that Britain is a safe place to live and walk at night. 'Why are civilised people behaving in an uncivilised manner in a civilised society like people in developing countries?' what a confused society. When did civilised and rich citizens of Britain become petty criminals?

What a shameful act, Britain government against military government in Nigeria. Yet some British bankers linked to late dictator Sani Abacha on $4 billion stolen from the federal republic of Nigeria. It was found that 42 accounts held at 23 banks in the UK had a turnover of £0.87 billion in 1996 – 2000. We cannot understand why the British government is still taking stolen money from developing country. 'Is the developing country stolen money a source of wealth to Britain?' 'You gave us £20,000 in aid but indirectly take millions from our economy.' 'Is the money you are giving developing country an interest from their stolen money in British banks?' Nigeria repatriates more than $2 billion from UK, USA and Switzerland and among other counties. Britain supporting military government that overthrew a democratic elected government – the Nigeria military Government that claimed to solve Nigeria's problem and develop Nigeria are now under developing Nigeria's society. 'Developing Nigeria military officer's under-developing Nigerian developing economy why?' British government supporting semi military democracy, the ex-military officers or the family members or friends are still holding top positions in the house of senate or representative. 'Ex-military officers still under-developing Nigerian undeveloped economy.' 'Britain gives Nigeria 4 million mosquito nets and 40 million vaccinations to fight malaria – news in the British newspapers. Britain, you must be joking, I must try to see those net in my village once I reach Nigeria to believe that you are telling the truth, can any minister tell me which area in Nigeria the nets are distributed. Nigeria, the sixth largest oil producer in the world is what Britain is claiming to give free mosquito net. 'Britain helps in under developing Nigeria economy with Nigeria ex-military officers – why Europeans under-developing Africa developing economy. 'The Africa Military under-developing it's developing society with the western nation's support why?' With one son of the former British prime minister being in jailed in Africa against overthrown of a central government in Africa, we now know that Britain has been involving and gaining in military rule in Africa. If Britain's banking authority says no to stolen money, I think no stolen money will come to Britain from developing countries. Britain government is claiming it is Nigeria's internal problem but wants Nigerian government to help in terrorist fight against Britain's society. 'But how can British bankers which help undeveloped Nigerian economy, develop the same Nigerian economy now?'

Seeing Nigerian streets, it may sound unbelievable that some of the beautiful buildings in London, Dubai, Singapore and many other cities in the United States of America are owned by Nigerian past and present leaders, leaving Nigeria to decay in each given year. 'Nigeria military regimes that used beatings, arbitrary arrests, censorship and intimidation to rule by fear, human rights groups said the regimes has committed multiple human rights violations and was illegal and yet, Britons still doing business with the regimes indirectly – telling the public one thing and doing a different thing. Britons confused about saying no to the regimes because of the nation oil – what a confused society.' In addition, Sudanese military personnel is being trained in Britain and war items sold to them despite Britain's criticism of the regime's butchery in Darfur, British government telling the public one thing and doing a different thing. 'I thought civilised societies should be a teacher to uncivilised society and their vision is to see developing nations change and for its people to experience the goodness of civilisation.' Why companies from a rich and civilised British dumping toxic waste in Africa? Toxic shame – The shadowy history of a slick British oil giant as thousands injured after toxins dumped in African city – thousand suffered short-term illness, including vomiting, diarrhoea, and more serious including miscarriage, still births, and birth defects. Now, Britain trading giant agrees to pay millions to Africa victims maimed and scarred by dumping of polluted sludge in Africa. 'Still an unanswered question – why are repressive Africa regimes given the succour of British aid?' Photographs of capture Saddam Hussein, a prisoner in British newspaper and dead bodies of Saddam Hussein and sons and Abu musab al-zarqawi killed in war front in British newspaper – yet they were captured or killed at war front. Saddam Hussein's gold gun was seized at UK Heathrow airport and packages marked as computer equipment, stolen by British soldiers. It is no more fighting war against uncivilised ruler but instead taking Iraq's valuable items for personal gain. Thief soldiers in British defence like in developing countries of Africa and Asia. Where is the stolen Saddam Hussein's gold gun and cigar case? We are in confused society.

A British girl 7-years-old starves to death by his parents, mother 33, and stepfather 29 in Birmingham city. The little girl and her sibling were so hungry that they go to their neighbour's garden to steal bread put out for birds in a rich and civilised British society. The girl, her sisters and brothers were found by a social worker lying on mattresses in the squalid room at their home undernourished and quiet. The social worker did not do a follow-up check. Their parents were arrest and charged with causing or allowing her death by neglect. Even a civilised society with state child and other benefit system in crisis. British parent in a civilised and rich society has no food to feed its children. We are in a confused society.

The events of the America credit crunch and the Northern rock bank customers' anxious queue to empty their account with the crisis-hit bank, some customers have queued for days looking and behaving like people in the third world country. More than 300,000 people queued to get their money, more than £2 billon cash was taken out in three days even with the assurance and guarantee from the British prime minister and chancellor. 'I thought money is safe in civilised society once you buy share in a registered company like North rock bank, I miss my money' I shouted. Can civilised people behave like uncivilised society in 21st century British society? What a confused society. Why is money in banks and shares in companies not safe in civilised society? Money and shares crisis, an uncivilised act in uncivilised societies is now in civilised society of Britain and USA – I lost my money in both countries. Why British rich and civilised society still having huge deficit in funding pensions of Britain's workers? What a confused society. A British bank worker has been found guilty of £500,000 bank sting by helping fraudsters defraud her wealthy customers out of their accounts. The bank worker leaked vital details including dates of birth and account passwords from the Barclays Bank computer system to the thieves. Who then pose as real customer and ripped the best accounts vast sums of money from the bank only splashing it out on expensive jewelleries and holidays – acts mainly seen in developing and uncivilised Society? A British firm also gave Arabian prince a four-engine aircraft as part of the arms deals however; politicians stop the fraud investigation by independent government agency – corruption, criminal activities in 21st century in British society. Another British oil trader was accused of paying millions of pounds in bribes to Saddam Hussein's officials to export oil in return for humanitarian and food goods. The British trader conned the £32 billion United Nations oil-for-food scheme via fixing the oil price by bribing Iraqi officials. So people from civilised society do give and take bribes and can defrauded developing country as to get rich. 'Britain government openly pretend to be helping a country while Briton carryout some defraud from the offices.' Why is the world business partner you could do without from the civilised society of United States of America? 'Bernard Madoff' the former chairman of the NASDAQ stock exchange conned thousands of investors nearly $65 billion. He's now serving life in prison. Where has all the monies gone? A civilised society like US has the world most conned man, what a shameless society, what a confused society.

The world's longest rider, who pedalled round the globe for 44 years and 350,000 miles had his bike stolen in Britain and the bike were later found abandoned in a local park. Another cyclist who pedalled 5,000 miles across the world only had his bike stolen when he got home to Britain, The cycle survived bandits and being left unlocked in slum-undervaluing countries but was stolen in Britain's civilised society. When did Britain become a nation of petty criminals? In year 2008, a top British party leader has become Britain's latest crime victim after thieves made off with his mountain bike while he shopped in a Portobello road supermarket. In 2008, over 17,700 bikes were reported stolen in London city and 530 thousand bikes estimated to have been stolen nationwide this year – has your bike gone missing in London city? Rush to Brick Lane's black market, it may well end up being hawked at Brick Lane market on a Sunday morning in the East End. Those of high-profile figures end up at internet online marketing. 'When did a civilised British society become a nation of thieves?' What a confused society.

New report says that one in eight sick days taken by British workers are fake, sick days taken on Monday or Friday to award themselves long weekend. Have I learnt any good behaviour in this Britain's confused society of 21st century?

London police are responsible for more than three road accidents in London every day that is about 21 to 25 accidents in each given week. Britain's police kill one innocent person, unconnected with any chase and crime in every 10 days by crashing their cars during chasing, a force that is suppose to help in avoiding accidents. 'Britain's police top in the world say the British media – you British media people must be kidding and confused. One ethnic assistant commissioner of police from London metropolitan police authority claims of 30 discrimination allegations in the force. 'Even police force faces allegations of discrimination, what a confused society.' An innocent Brazilian was shot dead by British police expert shooters after being mistaken for a suicide bomber. British police convict by old bailey jury of exposing the public to risk. Metropolitan police commissioner chief and other officers refuse to resign. It's shocking that even Britain's police not gangs can misuse firearms leading to a fatal shooting of a Brazilian in Britain. 'A civilised society police force in a confused state of taking order for the use of fire arms, what a confused force.' Another white British farmer, a dad of three was given a kung fu-style kicking by two police cops who thought he was a joy rider fleeing with a stolen car that he lost 60 per cent vision in his eyes and bruising to his head, ribs and back. How many apologies from Britain's police this year for making mistakes in the carryout of their tasks. Why do we blame our present teenage shooting generation, since we have a confused police force? In addition, a British man planned and hires hit men who murdered his police officer wife to get £367,000 insurance and ran off with his girlfriend was jailed for life. The police officer knew that the man is a son of a suspected double killer and he had a first marriage, which ended by his first wife paying him off to end their hellish marriage, the police officer normally use her rank to recover money for her husband's escort agency. Why should a police officer marry a criminal and a son of criminal, still many questions to answer between British police and criminal gang relationship, why white crime in civilised society police force? What a confused society? A lucrative Scotland Yard metropolitan police authority awarded contracts to friends of top police officer, an act you see in an uncivilised society in Britain's society. CORRUPTION and BRIBERY even in a civilised British society police force of 21st century. We are in confused society? Do not call British police for help about yobs behaviour – 'low level' anti-social behaviour and hooliganism said top police officer? Yobs issues are the local council responsibility, 'when has bad behaviour not the main cause of crime in our community?' Yet the public keep calling police station for 95 percent of the public do not know what yobs behaviour is – what a confused society. However, when did British police stop support-managing community related disability issues? When is anti-social behaviour and hooliganism low in level – a mother and disabled daughter called police more than 30 times in five years about the youths abuse to them and police did not do anything than issues a warning letters to young thugs and later they were hounded to death by the same group of yobs – a mother killed her disable daughter and herself. The pair suffered years of verbal abuse, stone-throwing and vandalism however, police officers were said to have failed to link or prioritise the pair complaints by the inquest. 'The police office visiting the estate for the pair complaints often just chatted to youths, failing to see their behaviour as criminal for the five years period.' 'Police allowed teen yobs or teen gangs – 'British Street rats' to torment a mum and her disabled daughter to death.' The inquest of a mother and her disabled daughter death, said it now the responsibility of the local councils to control anti-social behaviour since a law change in 1996 and the area council apology for not passing and managing the family information with police well. The inquest said the mother was driven to kill by stress and anxiety over her daughter's future and anti-social behaviour and said the death was unlawfully killed. The police issued an unreserved apology and later said there are things we did have done differently with the council – after the pair death. What a confused society as the local council departments could not work together with the police in a civilised society of British 21st century to save life. Are we not in a confused society? The British home office secretary says, 'police must get tough on violent yobs, police officers claiming that anti-social behaviour is no longer a police matter, that it's for local authorities, is ludicrous and ridiculous. The minister criticised police officers who fail to tackle anti-social behaviour and hooliganism, however did not mention that the councils has failed their community. So are anti-social behaviour issues the task of the local authority with police support or the task of police with local authority support minister? Do the public follow home office minister or the police officers side? We are in a confused society.

What another confused civilised way of becoming popular in British society, a mother reported his son 19-years-old who burgled her house. Her and her son's pictures showed in all the British national newspapers and TV. Another two girls reported their mother to the police for drunk driving, the mother and daughters pictures showed in all the national newspapers and TV. Moreover, a dad found bullets in his son's bedroom and handed him to police, his and his son's pictures was shown in all the British national newspaper and TV. I hope this is not another confusing ways of some of the British families to try to become popular. I thought Britain has a good social welfare services that manages family affairs. Family becoming popular, famous and becomes an instant celebrities for reporting its members to police. Very soon, we'll have a charity organisation for families who report its members to police, so donation and grants comes in and the individual charity gets richer.

I went to a British seaside to buy fresh fish but they refuse selling the good-catch dead fishes to me but was going to dump or discard about one tonne '60 percent of their catch' of good fresh dead fishes to the sea. I asked the fish operator why he is discarding dead fishes back to the sea and he replied 'European Union quota system did not permit us to catch this type of fish.' My question is why they did not discard live fishes as they catch the fishes knowing that that type of fish is not in their quota. European fish quota system's aim to save some type of fish life, are causing more problems to cost of fish and non-availability of fish. However, this is a caught-dead fish I want to buy, I need fish and you are discarding dead fishes to sea, it is bad. May be the British fish operators thought I was an E U inspector and pretending to cover their cunning behaviour of catching and selling unquote fishes of the European Union. Poor confused villagers.

A civilised society where its citizens do carry out benefit fraud, about £135 million Fraud of benefit claims in 2006/07, £25 million in housing benefits, £3.8 million in income support and more than 16,000 disabled parking badges being used by people who do not need them. Can a civilised society behave in this way? State benefit was given to civilised people for 7 days period but they spent it on alcohol and drugs in three hours and then stay poor for 6 days before the next benefit payment day then start committing crime – shoplifting. I call this group of Britons RICH BUT POOR BRITONS, having state benefit but remain poor. In Britain's civilised society where father 65-year-old, mother 64 years, their children 40 and 38-year-old, and grandchildren 19, 18, 16-years-old are sharing drugs together, all depending on state benefit and have no other recreational activity than drugs and alcohol misuse. Is this type of family among the civilised British society? A British father raped his own daughter from her 11-years-old to her 25-years-old 800 times, once in each given week as to get her pregnant so she will be able to claim more state benefit – a child benefit. He raped his daughter for 16 years, makes his own daughter a sex slave at their living home in Scotland. She fell pregnant six times but had four miscarriages, one stillbirth and her other survived for only eight months. Just for child benefit a father rapes and makes his daughter pregnant, I am in state of confused mood and in a confused society. British society has been betrayed by justice – a father having made her daughter become pregnant six times was jailed for only 3 years, what a shame. 'African children must be grateful you have well-respect fathers.' Is Britain's and Europe's civilised society, what is a civilised society? What good have I learnt from this confused society.

Britain is a rich successful society but rude and always moaning - a third world behaviour. Where Britons leaders are hopelessly corrupt indirectly – it is call white colour crime in Britain but called crime in developing countries. Parliamentarians bribed to pass counter terrorism bill of 42 days detention. Honours given out in return for a donation, another mystery donation of millions funding row to members of parliament, ministers and opposition leaders for the campaign and labour party boss quits. Members of Britain house of parliamentary and ministers claiming bogus homes that they did not live in. Politician's homes deal – my money, my tax, and our taxes. 'Sir, thanks for you have taught me a survival idea – master.' A cabinet minister resigned after claiming that he made an innocent mistake on his failure to declare donation for his election campaign. 'Failure to declare £103,000 the minister used for campaign is more than an innocent mistake.' I was in front of the cabinet minister's working building to see the face of the minister in case I made an innocent mistake in my working place but the minister left via the back door. 'Still many unanswered questions by the British government, arrangement for the donation of hefty sums and thousands of pounds without giving their identities by some contractors and some Britain companies for individual campaign of politicians.' The contractors later get contracts in exchange for their donation, bribes in 21st century society, I have learnt a new way of getting my ways out of business. Another member of parliament apologised for misusing his staffs' allowance of £50,000' to employ his two sons as researchers while they were full-time students. Britain's postal vote scandal, behaviours like that of the hypocritical third world rulers. I am just laughing at how MPs are all getting away with their expenses scandal as if we are in a third world nation. 'MPs hit by angry public backlash – party leaders beg for forgiveness to the society as MPs put their names to remove the house speaker for the first time in more than 300 years.' A lot of uncivilised behaviour in Britain but where is the real civilised society? 'Honourable members are now criminal and fraudsters, where have the honourable title gone?' Parliamentary members resigned not jail and some members told to replay thousands of pounds, also the MP may not be facing fraud investigation for MP's expenses scandal, why? I am a bit confused, 'if frauds are not appropriate for the public, why frauds are appropriate for the politicians? 'MPs told to repay dodgy expenses but the taxpayer were being kept in dark about which ones were guilty – every MP has received a private letter telling them whether or not they should refund the public purse for alleged cheating, from extravagant gardening to wrongful mortgage claims.' Now, MP's claim expenses scandal, sex harassment and sex discrimination has removed honourable title from honourable members, I am a bit confused on what title name to use to address the MPs.

Britain a nation of moaning, if Britain losses international football matches, Britons start moaning, and claiming it is because of foreigners 'coloured people' in British football team, yet Britons are playing in foreign teams. The comments are not from the street homeless people but from the ministers, members of parliament, media executives etc. Britain's population is increasing, Britons start moaning, and claiming it is cause by foreigners-immigrants coming to Britain, yet many Britons are in other countries working. Moreover, young British girls are falling pregnant as to get high state benefit and better support services. Young British girls having more children from different husbands, for at least one among her husband's may be good and offers more cash to the lady plus her benefits, so increase her standard of living. British teenager's getting pregnant not because they do not know how to get access to Britain's free contraception treatments, so they can get access to state social benefit and housing benefit. 'England is the divorce capital of Europe – headline news in all the British national newspaper.' Some Britons claiming and moaning that their present 21st century housing problems are caused by immigrants, many houses are being taken by foreigners. If British society economy starts facing loss, Britons start moaning, and claiming it is because of foreigners working and sending their money back home, yet British companies are making billions of pounds in developing countries. 'Yet more than 4 million British living and working in other countries and sending their money home.' If British society starts facing employment problems, Britons start moaning, and claiming it is caused by foreigners working in Britain and yet a lot of Britain's industrial sectors are closing down because they cannot compete with other countries and yet many British people are working abroad. If British society is having huge benefit problem, Britons start moaning, and claim is caused by refugees and foreigners claiming state benefit, yet more white Britons are claiming more state benefit. Britons government, keep moaning on all society issues are discredit to Britain's society and discomfort to foreigners in Britain. Should I stay in Britain and suffer depression or should I go back to Nigeria with shame. Many of the Austrians, Americans and Europeans come to London to work for three to five years and go back to their countries but Africans and Asians come to work, born, buy houses, open businesses compete with white Britons and become British citizens. I am among the foreigners white British society is moaning at, should I stay or go back to Africa? What a confused society. Whatever people from ethnic minority do white Britons must moan? Why is Britain a nation of moaners?

Is civilised society just use of modern electrical and music systems, a society that uses new science and technology items is advanced of another society. How can medical doctor in a British hospital have six tattoos in arms and piercing in ears and a female doctor have six bodies piercing in her ears and one in her nose (studs) – it is a sickening behaviour, this type of civilised culture is not for medical doctors? A teacher with eight tattoos, body branding and six bodies piercing in ears and nose, what is he going to teach children - Bad habits 'body branding, tattoos and piercing'. A British primary schoolteacher is a secret sex dominatrix. In the day time, she is a school teacher for 5 – 6 years-old but at night time she dish out physical education with a difference doing depraved sex sessions, involving physical touching and playing human sex parts in the public – armed with riding crops, belts, whips and canes. Dominatrix sex sessions, it is all teaching we agree but not for respected British primary schoolteacher. A teacher is a sex dominatrix, what good have I learnt in this civilised society. A university student girl with four studs in each ear – total eight earring studs, one nose stud, one mouth stud, large body tattoos and red/blue coloured hair. What a shame in a civilised society. A male police officer with five tattoos on his arms and ear piercing-stud, just like ex-mentally offender or a criminal, he must have had mental related issue and need treatment. A police officer with tattoos all over his body, the police officer has not committed any criminal act but the fashion did not represent a police officer's, I thought police officers are supposed to look decent in their apparels. Some British civil servants looking like superman and woman or event promoters-bouncers with their body tattoo in government offices in 21st century British society. Some workers in the office with rings in 10 fingers, wearing six earring (ear stud) in each ear and about six anklets or bangles in each hand – is body tattoos, wearing toe rings, nose studs, and body piercing and brandy a civilised fashion. If yes, the body brandy/tattoos, and mouth, tongue, and nose studs British are the ugliest and weirdest I have seen in British society. 'Self-harm (body branding, tattoos and piercing) mentally related issue comes in many ways and sizes, and is now a fashion in civilised society.' Tattoos-body harm is now a fashion, whatever you do in a civilised society is the best and most civilised lifestyle.

Year 2007 British chancellor says Britain's economy is the strongest in the developed countries and fast growing economy among developed countries. 'Britain's wobbling economy; America's credit crunch makes the British society to cry.' With American credit crisis which has increased, making Britain's home repossession orders to soar 165 per cent in some area. About 120,000 repossessions will take place in year – 2008. 'Americans use toilet room without cleaning well, Britain nation smell rotten.' Americans cough or sneeze, without covering their mouth or nose with their hand, Britain follows America and catch germs panic. 'America gets credit crunch issues, Britain get credit war issues.' 'America has economy problem, Britain lost. America gain, Britain lost, why?' British people check telephone boxes to find out if there were any coins left in them and eat from rubbish bins – are they among rich and civilised British society. Chancellor, which Britain economy is the strongest; whom do you think you are kidding or force pretending to cheat. Where British poverty children's family cannot provide after school textbooks for their children to read at home, school uniform, or take breakfast before going to school. 'Violence against British babies and young children under ten year old are in increase and likely reason was increasing stress in families suffering from economic and work pressure.' With about 30 per cent of children live below poverty line in some British council homes because their unemployed parents are relying solely on benefit handouts. Britain, why not solve you internal problems before solving Iraq's problem? A British council worker died in absolute poverty after losing his home - flat and has no money as a result, started living in an 8ft by 4ft cupboard for six months, died in the cupboard. Britain, a Rich society which eats bad foods 'buy one and get one free offers' intensive chicken farm 'indoor, battery, and cage' farming – why not free range chicken farming. Intensive chicken farming 'dirty, cheap, fatty, and tasteless chicken' main for war societies, is now the main food source for rich civilised society.' I am now eating buys one and gets one free, cheap and unsafe food, should I continue to stay or go home. I thought

Britain is a rich society as mentioned by British chancellor, 'just an Englishman speaking English is not an achievement. What will be my future when I become old in Britain's society and cannot work, without a joint family and delay in getting into benefit system then I will start checking phone boxes for money? I must be fighting and killing to get food when I am old and could not work. Should I stay in Britain and face depression or should I go to Nigeria and bury my head in shame? 'A homeless eastern European man 21-years-old was jailed for hitting two students with bottle and stole their shopping. Both girls suffered head wounds. The man told police that he carried bottles for protection and admitted stealing the shopping because he wanted food, an European wounding people for a meal in 21st century European society, what a shameful act.' In addition, eating from the rubbish bins in developing countries may be call to be a poor way of living and the developing countries will be criticised by developed country media for not taking good care of its citizens. Now eating from rubbish bin in developed country has a big English word or name called FREEGAISM – meant being able to eat fat better freely from rubbish than when we were forced to buy food from shops. Developed country claimed as one best way of eating well. Developing country does it is uncivilised way of doing things and not good, but when developed country does the same; it is good and most civilised way. 'I have seen poverty and richness married together, civilised society eating from rubbish bins officially, bins for freegaism blue in colour at backs of some supermarkets.'

It is intimidating seeing America and Britain live on television going to war with Iraq, even when the United Nation Organisation are saying 'NO' to going to war with Iraq. 'Uncivilised road to peace, 20/03/2003 America's missiles hit innocent target in Baghdad marking the start of the American and British led invasion even before 01/05/2003 United Nations security council authorises US-led administration in Iraq.' Why, Britain and America in politics of death over Iraq's oil? Why America and Britain didn't claim that the war and problem with Iraq was not a religious issue but war between uncivilised rulers and civilised rulers, why didn't America and Britain think that they are civilised society but fought Iraq, a deliberate act of provocation and harassment to Iraq's innocent society to give up their wealth - oil? Who are the main contractors in Iraq now? My Iraqi family friends lost their parents, their home destroyed and lost their family business to foreign companies – myself or my society might be next to be destroy. Is the war for weapons, race, oil, or using fear of terrorism as excuses for a dangerous brand of economic protectionism to other countries, an excuse to improve America and Britain's economy? 'At least half the children in Iraq have dropped out of school because of violence and there's more poverty in the war-torn country.' Where are the American and British civilised leaders? After the Iraqi war, I knew that civilised society or their politicians are helpers from hell, lying about their motive to end military rules in Iraq. 'Americans and British are all liars and hypocrites who are only interested in the riches and resources of Iraq.' American and British governments as a whole gave the public false and inflated expectation of Iraqi weapons that caused the war. Therefore, America and Britain have no self-respect for Iraq society, force pretending to be helping but are there to mislead the Iraq society for their wealth and oil. 'I am now mastering the way to be useful to myself, through cunning behaviour.' Today millions of Iraqis are homeless and refugees in another country and thousands of innocent Iraqis and Britons killed by politicians telling false information to gain Iraqi oil wealth. If civilisation is the higher advance of society on science and technology, why Iraq can not be allowed to develop their own science and technology – weapon. Can an uncivilised society develop weapons that can be more effective to that made in America or Britain civilised society? Why America and Britain ask countries to refuse selling items to Iraq that may be use for making of weapons instead of fighting Iraq? America and Britain removed Saddam Hussein, yet Iraqi streets are still not safe, to establishment of peace and order or a sense of democracy means you betrayed yourselves - America and Britain. Iraq has become a more and more dangerous country, overran by gangs of marauding religious fanatics, Iraq in terrible violence. I thought Iraq would be in peace like American or British societies after the war. 'American and British politicians are to be blamed they started the war not the faith fighters.' Iraq war a 'waste of lives' – still no closer to getting the economy on its feet, wiping out religious fanatics or corruption due to lack of resources after 7 years. Some legend societies like Untied States of America and Untied Kingdom are not just born to be legends. However, they are immortal for everlasting fame – even after Iraq war, UK and USA are not blocked by the rest of the world. What a confused world.

British disturbing new figures show that alcohol-related deaths have doubled in just ten years. The average British age of those dying has plummeted, is this civilised culture – Britons drink, get drunk and end up in a street gutter. Britons drink, get drunk, carried away and unconscious. Britons drink, get drunk and openly have sex in the street. Britons drink, get drunk and sleep on dance floor or street corridor. Britons drink, get drunk and the streets becomes your toilet room. Britons drink, get drunk and start street fighting and end up in the hospital. Britons drink, get drunk and stagger from club to the street with handbag and shoes in hand. Britons drink, get drunk, become legless and being loaded into a car from fall over on street pavement with sore head and provide work to the hospital. Britons drink, become drunk, dash out and get a criminal record. Britons drink and become drunk, aggressive and lose your senses, help to fill British hostels and provide work to the British society. Britons drink and get drunk, keeps running wild and keep embarrassing your country on holidays aboard. Each alcohol addict cost the taxpayer-myself at least £500,000 in their lifetime. My future generation or I cannot follow this type of civilised British society of 21st century alcohol culture. Why don't people of civilised British society know what is good and bad for their body. If a Briton needs to drink or eat out in restaurant he goes for a new credit or debits card, need a drink get new credit cards. Cash machine cards are being issued to children as young as 11-years-old by banks without their parental consent. I have read Britain's history - back in 1906, hospital patients putting away their share of alcohol. In absence of antibiotics, brandy is giving as a painkiller and stout prescribed for medicinal purposes and patient smoking in the wards was seen as a way of killing germs. With the present British alcohol and drug culture, is Britain going back to 1906 society and is 1906 society the main British civilised society we have been hearing as a well-behaved and civilised society. 'If we have civilised tribes, communities or regions then, where are this civilised societies.' I think the word – uncivilised society is just Prejudice – the desire to look for a scapegoat.

British's aggressive foreign behaviour led to a lot changes to different society and ENGLISH-England become master of the entire world with their English language. England's people spread English, English the highest spoken language and making other society language second-class language. If I do not speak English, I will not be dreaming of visiting Britain. Now that English people's aggressive policy and behaviour has attracted more foreigners, you have to bear with the problems your granddad caused; do not be confused why many foreigners are in Britain-London city. 'Little master England, commonwealth nation's grownup.' Yet Britain still shows aggressiveness to other countries in present 21st century, British and American companies have secured series of multi-million-pounds from Iraqi oil contracts in the country's eight biggest oil field, fuelling criticism, the war was largely over Iraqi fuel reserves. I thought Britain said that the war was not for Iraqi oil and now you are doing oil business in Iraq – Britain and America, you are confused society. Britain, you wanted and encouraged Africans and Asians into Britain in the past and now you call us illegal immigrants and put a barrier on our entering. Britain, you wanted us in the first instant. In 1948, the British nationality act conferred the state of British citizen on the entire commonwealth subjects. We still belong to commonwealth nations' club, 'for the mother country related issues' now you are downgrading commonwealth membership to improve European relationship. Yet we have foreign high commissions and not embassy's, when are we going to share our club cakes and end the club meetings, take us or end the club meeting because it is not a civilised way to treat past partners? Even in 21st century, a French politician was arrested and charged with trying to smuggle 16 Vietnamese migrate into Britain in the back of van packed with shrimp noodles from the France northern ports to the south coast of England. The migrants, who were thought to have paid for their passage in cash, were sent back to France. What a great embarrassment to the French authority, what a confused Europe society.

I thought the most trained, experienced and qualified workers take the top jobs in government and public sectors in a civilised society. In 21st century British society, you get jobs via connection; the unqualified workers take the best jobs, an act you see in developing country or uncivilised society is now in civilised Britain's 21st century society. British, you brought education to many countries and you now have less regard for education, mostly black people university education is no more consider as been a talent. 'White Britons faced with a choice between unskilled or unqualified white Briton and black Briton with skilled, qualified and experienced in work. Broadly speaking you will take the white person and merely end-up ruining things for black Britons keen to learn.' I am still hanging my university certificate in my room wall, thus ending university education for people who have no job connection. About 85 percent of killed teenagers in Britain with knife and gun are from black community and how many black adults are in prison; in a society black people make less than 10% of the population, some hopeless black people try to strike back on the society for survival caused by discrimination in the society. So a lot of the black people end up in the prison as they try to make their living condition better and many stay at home and suffer from depression and other mental related issues as they think and future become hopeless to them.

Britain, you introduce Christianity to African societies and destroy their gods and cultures. Britons you destroy Africa god figures in their community however, I am seeing ancient bizarre figures in exhibits at British museums. 'Our ancient cultures are alive and thriving with modern civilised society of Britain – then what is civilised society?' Why did early European Christians destroy Africa gods in the 19th century and now the gods are alive in the 21st century Britain society. We are in confused society. Some British offices with gay and lesbian symbols refused Christian or Muslim symbols, gay and lesbian people claiming being discriminated against while some organisations have 95 per cent of their company work force from gay and lesbian group. UK, why did you destroy Africa traditional gay and lesbian lifestyles via early Christianity to native Africans? 'British workers who take Christian beliefs into work practice can end up in a disciplinary hearing. Why?' I thought Britain is Christian faith nation. You brought Christianity to Africans and destroyed their gods and culture, when did British people becomes a nation of multiple faiths? British Bishop's embarrassing homosexuality (gay/lesbian), saying he will be in gay (man-to-man sex) relationship for life. He believes the mystery of covenanted love can work between men or between women of the same sex. Being a gay, he is a symbol of hope for an awful lot of gay people, say British new Bishop. The male Bishop has a male partner for the past 27 years – I thought homosexuality was ancestral behaviour and not modern civilisation's behaviour. Should I go back and start worshipping my tradition gods. I thought a Christian leader cannot discriminate against anybody but cannot preach the benefit of homosexuality when Christians believe it is against the word of God. 'Civilised society embarrassing gay and lesbian lifestyle, where will all the newborn babies come from?' Another British church rector said he has no regrets about performing a gay-man to man marriage at his historic London church. Two homosexual priests who lives in the same church are gay and having man-to-man marriage conducted for them by another priest who lives in the same church. Now many Britons do not attend church services but use church buildings as private resident's flats, commercial offices and homeless hostels. British people you teach our society about traditional Christian family value but you're now having a lot of broken family – divorces. Do you want my society to move back to our practice - a man marring up to five to ten wives, woman marring men, women marring women, men marring men before Europeans visited Africa? What good news from Africa that 'a South Africa businessman going back to traditional Africa culture by marries four women at the same time on august 2009.' However, in the 21st century, Britons still dating and having children from 2 to 4 women the same time and claiming they are his partners not his wives, why? 'A British dad got a 15-year-old girl and his wife pregnant in the same month. While the mums-to-be were expect their baby, the shameful father, who has twelve kids with seven women, was languishing in jail for having sex with another girl. What a confused society.

You brought and encouraged industries to my society but now you are moving your industries to other countries – developing countries, what is wrong with your country? I have come to Britain to use 'Britain's Philips made items but what am seeing in British stores is Philips made in china.' 'I still have my British made rover car in Nigeria but need also a British made rover car in London city but what am seeing is china made rover cars.' When is made in Britain coming back? Are you moving from civilised to uncivilised society, backward society master Britain?

I am seeing the British culture with some uncivilised events now and having a bit of laughter and a little bit of silly abuses on the British society. Britain a nation of animal lovers, that is our belief compared to countries where they whip donkeys to death and eat cat or dogs. However, in Britain, tiger skin, polar bear rugs and ivory brushes, rare bird egg sold in British market and dogs dumped in parks with wound suggesting it might have been involved in an organised fight or due to victim's cruelty in 21st century British animal lover's society. Is dogs racing and fighting events, a civilised way of making use of dogs? A picture of a belly dancer with a passion for snakes is still adding to her collection despite already having 45 snakes in British national newspaper. She live in a flat with 46 snakes as pets – how can a person who keeps and punish 46 snakes in one room be a snake lover? What a confused society. In Britain, a litter of five-weeks-old kittens were saved from being crushed in a refuse lorry after dustmen collecting rubbish found the kittens dumped in a bin bag – animal lover British society act. An abused 6 years monkey was left severely deformed after 5 years in

2-meters cage saved from a flat. The monkey could not climb, as his bones had not formed properly. The monkey was hunched and unable to stand after a decade in windowless room with just a TV for company. Monkey watching TV for 8 hours in each given day, that must be civilised monkey, is why Britain is nation of animal lover. What a confused society. Whatever you do in a civilised society is the most civilised ways of doing things. Another, thirty-four dead horses, ponies, and donkeys found in Buckinghamshire, Britain. The animals died because of neglect and were left where their bodies fell in the field – just like Africa and Asia societies do. A daughter (medical doctor) who spent 40 years helping her father and mother run their farm valued £1.5 million was given nothing but their £1.5 million properties was given to animal care organisation – this is why Britain is a nation of animal lover. Is this behaviour a civilised way to act? A Briton 26-old-years man who stabs his dog to death after receiving a job rejection letter has been jail for killing his dog. In addition, a 27-years-old Briton let his dog starve to death because she was too tired to look after it. She starved the dog to death after locking it in a bedroom for three weeks because she was having training. Another Briton claimed his neighbour's cat was a menace and looks pleased after breaking in and knocking over a vase in his room. He punched the cat unconscious and then hurled it into a river to die and said that he did so because the animal was a bully. That must be a civilised way of killing dogs and cats than killing it for meat like people from uncivilised society that eat dogs and cats. One wonder if it is better to kill cats or dogs for fun in one society or for human consumption in another society, which of the society is animal lover? As a frontline and community outreach worker, 'I have seen the best and worst of British people keeping animals in their homes.' Most of the world is far crying for banned on whaling, is whale banning a civilised way or behaviour of loving whales? Japanese kill whales and take not more than 10% of the body with the rest of the whale's body being thrown into the sea. Is Japanese whaling fleet a barbaric tradition or scientific research? 'Eco-whale pirates that is stopping the killing of whales versus a Japanese whale killing fleets, which of these societies or groups' behaviour is civilised? A whale in London River Thames died or was killed; skeleton kept in the London museum, the body used for experiment and the rest of the body thrown away as rubbish. Should each given country museums keep whale skeleton, how many whales will remain in the world? The poor southern part of Lembata Island, Indonesia kill whale, the whole community eat 95% of the whale during sea season, and skeleton thrown away as rubbish – Britain, there are more unused skeletons in Lembata seaside for your museum. Lembata Island or British museum which group is whale lover? Britain, a nation of animal lovers having a glamorising world record huge hunting animals on the TV and newspapers, what a shameful act. With Britons living and sleeping with dogs and cats in the same room or bed, feeding dogs with the best meat but are living in one bedroom flat with a dog and not walking the dog well, buying two chickens, one for him or her, and one for the dog or cat while some homeless people in the same area have no food. Another society that keep dogs in the yard for security and not allowing the dogs in the living and bed room but allows the dogs to live like animals and the dogs eat leftover foods – which group are civilised society and animal lover. 'I think it is not how long dogs live but how happy dogs live in their short stay.' Whatever you do in a civilised society is best way of doing things and most civilised way of acting. 'Should we feed our cat or dog first or the street homeless rough sleepers?' 'Is living in a flat and keeping a dog good behaviour, is the dog a prisoner or it has its own freedom in the flat rooms – should we keep dog if we live in a flat without a yard.' As a frontline and community outreach worker, I have seen the best and worst of British people in keeping animals as pet. I am a bit confused. 'British police arrested a Briton on suspicion of having sex with a sheep that is why Britain is a nation of animal lover.' How can Africa pygmy hedgehog that live happen in the busy pit be a house pet in Britain, 'I put them in cage, but they do have a habit of escaping and running round the house, you found them in cupboards, snuggled up in bed, and they even line up and watch the television at night', a pet lover claimed. Why British animal charities tell the public that they are causing more harm than good to the wild animals, help and send them back to the Africa bush pit native home for natural living since they are animal lovers. 'Wild animal lover, why not return the wild animals to their native home?' A crow was rescued from his nest after getting his leg caught in a piece of string and being left hanging upside down, it was more than two hours operation involving seven fire fighters, animal welfare officers and motor crane, wasting my/taxpayers' money. What a confused civilised society. Now, Britain as a nation of animal lover has taken a u-turn by a mother and son face jail after turning their home into a zoo by collecting unwanted pets free from people. They crammed 62 animals into a room, 20 birds in cramped cages, and a turtle in a cage with no UV light – ZOO FROM HELL. 'Who says wild animals look please in a zoo and human homes should think again.' An animal prosecutor told court that the animal room were very small and dirty and most of the animal had to be put down because of their poor condition – incidents of deliberate suffering to animals but claiming to be animal lover. What a confused society.

Drugs worth more than £100 million smuggled into British prisons in each given year caused by addicted prisoners corrupting prison staffs and British government showing more interest in managing the drug problem than eradicating it. What a shameful and embarrassment act to Britain's drug control agencies and prison agencies. What a confused society. British navy hunting South American smugglers seized 45 sacks of cocaine weighing 900 kg and worth £40 million. A civilised society claiming to be stopping hard drugs movements in other countries but cannot even control hard drug related issues in its own prison yards. British teenagers are the most drunks in the world and most cannabis users in the world. Deadly drugs like heroin and cracked cocaine are now cheaper than a can of beer. Prices has fallen because vast quantities of drugs are now being flown into Britain that kid are being hook on deadly habits for the price of a mere pocket money. 'Is substance dependency a civilised way of behaving?' Is British force pretending to be stopping or distributing hard drugs? 'A navy officer on warship hunting drug barons has been charged with trying to smuggle £1 million of cocaine into Britain.' 'British Royal Navel poison British communities why?' Britons has not stopped its home border drugs marketing why going for international drug trafficking control. Is British Royal Navel stopping or marketing drugs? Another, British Royal Navel Ship – HMS Iron Duke found more than five-and-a-half tonnes of the class 'A' drug after a fishing boat was spotted off the south America coast in an area known for trafficking. The ship made its largest cocaine seizure with a haul worth more than £240 million. However, the drugs problem at Britain's biggest prison is worth more than £1 million a year – the amount of drugs entering Wandsworth prison is fuelling gang violence, with corrupt prison officers among those to be blamed – with most illegal substance available to most inmates with money. What a confused society. Now, 'you discover drugs are cheaper than at home-Britain than other country unless you're in or from Colombia.'

Britain nation, British people, Africans thinks you are an angel. Once I reach Africa, will I consider myself civilised or uncivilised person with my education qualification and training in Britain, as I have not learnt any good but cunning behaviour in this society? At least in developing societies children have joy and liberty to move around freely, that science and technology cannot buy. I am still not nearer to knowing what has caused the British bad behaviour or what I called bad behaviour is just part of Britain's culture. It is shameful and an embarrassment to a civilised society. Yes, I think Britain is not any angel with British present alcohol and drug culture, gun and knife culture and divorce culture. The standard I was hoping to see fall down below what we-Africans have been hoping to see in Christianity way of life and general society behaviour. British televisions and newspapers are being filled with stories about youngsters and their involvement in crime, anti-social behaviour, extreme violence, two-third of robberies being committed by young people. British-born children are being trafficked for sexual exploitation, about 167 victims were rescued and 528 suspected traffickers were arrested in just six-months, police warned. Where have civilised British parents gone and where is the civilised society? Britain nation, a generation of fearful children, civilised society kids saying it is not safe without knife, no one fears you unless you have a knife. What a confused society. I am in a confused mood in Britain, a general society of fatal knifings, divorce, shooting, child sex abuse, human trafficking, and teenage parents etc, why are bad events increasing in each coming-given year in Britain's society? Where have the civilised individual Britons gone? The events are becoming so brutal, horrific and shocking that Britain may be considered being in a barbaric society. Who are those people behaving badly in Britain's civilised society? Why are civilised societies becoming confused societies? Some mothers with low-cut top revealing some angry-looking fallen apart breast and some with natural and surgery scars. Why shouldn't British children not behave like adults, use drug, drink alcohol, then carry knife and gun since the can easily see adult senses in the streets – we are just facing children alcohol, drug, gunning and knifing related issues and then the next children problem we will be facing will be raping caused by mums. Celebrities stripping off for charity and now are the public getting their kit off for a good cause. What a civilised charity society of death. 'You look great naked in public places.' It's so bad what our children are seeing in the public places. Naked for a good cause – naked charity calendar women, Naked for cancer support, Naked for anti-protest on global warming, Naked to end sectarian violence in football, Naked against eating meat in bid to encourage others to go vegetarian, Naked cyclists protest against cars, emission and aggressive drivers, Naked for rugby union and charity young care, Naked here and naked there, even dead human bodies are respected by not keeping them naked. What has charity got to do with nakedness and stripping of clothes in public area? A new British marketing promotion is, 'turn up in underwear in the shop floor and get a free outfit offer' backfires and police have been branded trouble maker for forcing more 100 bargain hunters queuing outside a London clothes shop in their underwear to cover up. The shopper's strippers off for a promotion at the new north London store of fashion which offered free outfits to the first 25 customers to turn up in their underwear from the streets. 'It's only a bit of fun – who's offended by us getting semi-naked – it's the same as being at the beach, the customers claimed as they wait out the shop semi naked for hours. What type of behaviour are children learning from this civilised society with common newspapers and TV stations showing all this naked images? 'Whatever you do in a civilised society is good, great and a civilised way of behaving, the consequence is increase in children behaving badly like adult.' How can a person look great naked in public places – where will our children go since nakedness has take control of our public places?

A civilised society who would not let uncivilised people to be civilised, it is not something I can be proud of when I reach Africa. How can I cope without the British society, going home, it is not easy? I am thinking of how to make my staying in Britain's civilised society a success, a civilised way of living with a quarter of white Britons now saying that they experience racial discrimination by social landlord and that new government figures have shown. What will a person from ethnic minority group expect with white Britons claiming that they being discriminated against? 'A white British vulnerable man cut off his own head with a chainsaw after being order out of his home to make way for developers.' What an uncivilised action in a civilised society. Should I stay in Britain living with a depressed health condition or should I go back to Nigeria and start living with hard conditions – what a confused thinking. Britain, how disappointing your society are now, having more community related disability issues than uncivilised-

African and Asian societies like alcohol and drug abuse, knifing and shooting, discrimination and corruption, child pornography and paedophile and priests openly accepting to be homosexuals. Why British children cannot move freely in their own community because of sex abuse, shooting and knifing in the society? So civilised society is about openly nude or naked walkers, strippers in lap dancing, bad comments, and etc. 'Whatever you do in a civilised society is the civilised and best way to behave.' Is this bad British behaviour new or has it been part of Britain's society culture? 'British ladies in prostitution – cash in hand first, then work or cash and carry for some minutes or hours.' Where is the British decent family society I have been hearing for years in Africa? 'Hope this night highway patrol ladies and men prostitutes must be foreigners.' Can a Briton behave in this type of lifestyle? I thought I was coming to see only decent families and society in Britain but I am in a confused society. I am a bit confused and disappointed. What story will I tell my uncivilised society when I reach home - Africa? Can there be uncivilised people in a civilised society? What is then civilised society? Why does Britain's civilised society behave so badly? What good behaviour have I learnt in this civilised society? Why experience uncivilised related issues in a civilised society, where have all the civilised individuals gone? 'How can killing and other crime activities be the most common joke and fun issues in the news in a civilised society?' What is the meaning of civilised society then? The unforgettable white people, the very white Britons, the masters of the universe – English. Master-Britain, your society has taught me nonsense but you are just unforgettable for good and bad. 'It's great to be here, it's great to be in Great Britain.' 'The best way to find out if a given civilised society is as impressive as the name sound is to go there and see for you.' I know what it is like on the streets in a civilised society. I am having a comfortable laugh, being in a civilised society and seeing people behaving in uncivilised manner is not funny but I have come to see Britain society and I have seen British people. People from developing countries stop running away from your country because civilised and uncivilised countries are the same so try and help your country to develop for civilised society has complex lifestyles with big opportunity and challenges, plan before leaving native home – are you up for it? English dictionary is confusing and making a mistake, the dictionary has gotten the meaning of civilised society wrong, 'civilised society as a society marked by refinement in taste and manners, cultured polished or society raised from barbarism to an enlightened stage of polished or sophisticated behaviour' – yet we are seeing people committing criminal activities in civilised society. Do we have civilised individuals in a given society and not a civilised society?

'When is Europe civilised society not civilised? Uncivilised issues developing in a civilised society, what is civilised society then?' People in a civilised society behave in an uncivilised manner, developing uncivilised issues, having uncivilised events, what is civilised society then? 'People from developing countries stop running away from your country because civilised and uncivilised countries are the same so try and help your country to develop.' Think decent living; think your native home support.